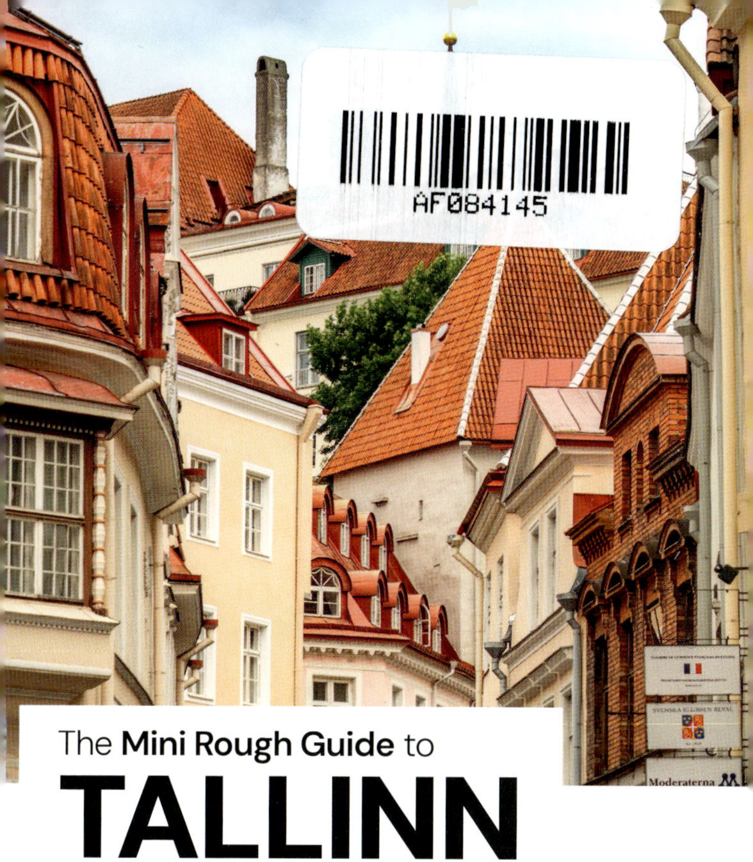

The Mini Rough Guide to
TALLINN

YOUR TAILOR-MADE TRIP
STARTS HERE

Tailor-made trips and unique adventures crafted by local experts

HOW ROUGHGUIDES.COM/TRIPS WORKS

STEP 1

Pick your dream destination, tell us what you want and submit an enquiry.

STEP 2

Fill in a short form to tell your local expert about your dream trip and preferences.

STEP 3

Our local expert will craft your tailor-made itinerary. You'll be able to tweak and refine it until you're completely satisfied.

STEP 4

Book online with ease, pack your bags and enjoy the trip! Our local expert will be on hand 24/7 while you're on the road.

PLAN AND BOOK YOUR TRIP AT
ROUGHGUIDES.COM/TRIPS

How to download your Free eBook

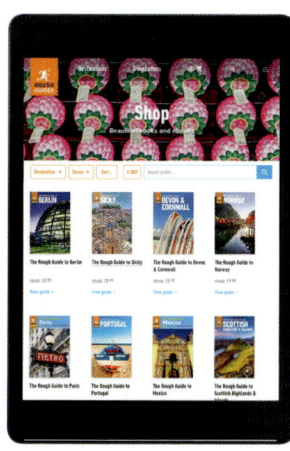

1. Visit **www.roughguides.com/free-ebook** or scan the **QR code** opposite

2. Enter the code **tallinn849**

3. Follow the simple step-by-step instructions

For troubleshooting contact: mail@roughguides.com

Contents

- **6** **Introduction**
  - **14** 10 Things not to miss
  - **16** A perfect day in Tallinn
  - **18** Tallinn on a budget
  - **20** Family-friendly Tallinn
- **22** **History**
- **33** **Places**
  - **33** Toompea
  - **46** Lower Town
  - **65** Parks and moats
  - **67** Kalamaja
  - **70** Kadriorg
  - **75** Outlying areas
  - **79** Excursions

- **93 Things to do**
  - 93 Culture
  - 94 Nightlife
  - 96 Shopping
  - 102 Sports and outdoor activities
  - 103 Children
  - 105 Festivals and events
- **107 Food and drink**
- **123 Travel essentials**
- **142 Index**

Introduction

Steeped in history, pulsing with energy and brimming with fairy-tale charm, Tallinn has earned its place among the must-see destinations of Europe. The city's soul is nourished by a progressive arts scene, the natural beauty of its parks and coastline, a buzzing nightlife and a post-Soviet edginess. All this, and the fact that it can be toured on foot, makes Tallinn an ideal choice for a city break.

WHAT'S NEW

Tallinn's markets are having a revamp. The recently renovated Balti Jaama turg (see page 78) has three levels of food, antiques, souvenirs and vintage clothing – you could easily spend a morning picking through Baltic snacks and decorative art, with a stop for coffee and *samsa* (filled pastries). Meanwhile, the Keskturg (Keldrimäe 9) – Tallinn's Central Market and the locals' favoured shopping haunt – is being jazzed up thanks to a new architect-designed hall, set to open in late 2025. The darling of Telliskivi Creative City, the 2019-opened Fotografiska Tallinn (see page 79) is a satellite of the popular Swedish gallery, where exhibitions centre on iconic images, Pop Art and surreal photography. In Kadriorg Park, the expanded Children's Museum Miiamilla (see page 105) is like a fairy-tale cottage discovered in the forest, with a hands-on music room, creative workshops and soft-play areas. Also in the park, near the swan pond, a striking new orangery (L. Koidula 34a) designed by local architects is a sprawling complex of local and exotic plants, including a winter garden and a permanent exhibition of butterflies and crickets. Over in the Noblessner Quarter, the Punctum Gallery (see page 70) is the latest addition to this former industrial enclave. The bright and airy arts space, set in a restored warehouse by the bay, is dedicated to contemporary works and photography by Baltic and Scandinavian upstarts.

The town hall tower in the heart of Tallinn's Old Town

This cosy city of just 460,000 inhabitants on the southern shore of the Gulf of Finland occupies an enviable position as a regional gateway. Its nearest neighbour, Helsinki, is less than ninety minutes away by ship, and Stockholm and St Petersburg can both be reached by overnight ferry. Latvia's capital, Riga, is a five-hour bus ride away.

Tallinn's role as a port-of-call goes back centuries. In fact, the port has been its defining feature since the early thirteenth century, when Danish troops and German crusaders invaded Estonia and laid the foundations of a major commercial hub. Soon after, Tallinn became a member of the Hanseatic League, an all-important association of medieval merchant cities. It grew rich in the fourteenth and fifteenth centuries as an intermediary in trade between the West and Novgorod in Russia. In the centuries that

The fortified gateway to Tallinn's bustling historic district

followed, the Swedish Empire, Russian Empire and Soviet Union each conquered this desirable harbour city, leaving their own mark on the urban landscape.

A MEDIEVAL MILIEU, A MODERN EDGE

Without question, Tallinn's most valuable treasure is its Old Town – a remarkable survivor from the Middle Ages. Encircled by a centuries-old city wall, it's a beguiling place of narrow streets and intimate squares, ancient houses and towering church spires.

Like no other place in Europe, the Old Town has somehow managed to cling on to its medieval atmosphere despite centuries of commerce, war and political change. The neighbourhood owes its survival in large part to a series of historic accidents. Economic downturns kept construction in check, and at critical junctures shrewd political settlements prevented the town from being sacked. The city's famous defensive ramparts, much of which is still intact, also helped a great deal in preserving the town for future generations. The area suffered from Soviet

> **NOTES**
>
> Tallinn is a popular destination for Finnish shoppers, particularly those after cheap deals on alcohol, which is heavily taxed in Finland.

bombing towards the end of World War II, and from some dubious reconstruction that followed, but the ensuing occupation also had at least one unexpected benefit: trapped in amber by the Soviet Union, Tallinn's Old Town escaped the overdevelopment inflicted on similar cities in the West.

Now for the most part restored to its original glory, the Old Town once again belongs to the world. In 1997, it was inscribed on the list of UNESCO World Heritage Sites.

> **WHEN TO GO**
>
> To make the most of Tallinn's brilliant summer weather, most visitors plan a trip around Midsummer, a three-day extravaganza of feasting, dancing and bonfires celebrated a few days after the solstice. High season also spans the Tallinn Fringe Festival, when music, dance and comedy performances take over the city's squares and markets in late August and September. Spring fever is palpable after Tallinn's long winter. The quieter shoulder season, spring also kicks off music mania with a string of festivals dedicated to jazz, classical, rock and choral music (the reason Tallinn is known as a UNESCO City of Music). Though days are short in the run-up to Christmas, Tallinn is awash in candlelight, sparkling decorations and holiday zeal (and soaked in spiced mulled wine, or *glögi*). Double down on the Christmas spirit with a day-trip to Helsinki, just two hours across the Gulf of Finland on a Tallink ferry.

But that's not to say the Old Town is a static museum piece – it is nothing of the kind. This is the heart of Tallinn, the hub of its eclectic restaurant scene and home to the city's famously raucous nightlife. Scattered among the fifteenth-century buildings are trendy cafés and bars. Town Hall Square, at the centre of the Old Town, is a destination for concerts, festivals and live performances. Bustling markets fill the streets. Crowds of foreign visitors add their own energy to the mix. And shopping here knows no limits. As ironic as it sounds, the Old Town is where the heart of modern Tallinn beats the strongest.

This captivating part of the city usually keeps visitors exploring for days, but as much as there is to see, limiting yourself to the Old Town would be a mistake. Within the city limits you can visit the

The lavish Baroque main hall in Kadriorg Palace

spectacular Kadriorg Palace, built for Russian Tsar Peter the Great; the museum ships of the Seaplane Harbour; beautiful Pirita Beach and River; the recreated farm villages at the Estonian Open Air Museum; and a scattering of curious Soviet-era constructions on the outskirts of town. Also, a string of relatively undiscovered cities not far from Tallinn offer fantastic day-trip opportunities and should not be passed up.

> **NOTES**
>
> Tallinn consistently rates as one of the most high-tech cities in Europe, and the country itself has been dubbed e-Estonia. In 2000, Estonia became the first country to declare internet access to be a human right.

HIGH-TECH AND HIGH-RISES

Despite being lumped in with its Slavic and Baltic neighbours by virtue of having been caught on the wrong side of the Iron Curtain, Estonia sees itself as having much more in common with Nordic countries. Indeed, the country's language and ethnic roots are Finno-Ugric, closely related to their cousins the Finns. Maybe it's not surprising, then, that Estonians, like the Finns and Scandinavians, tend to be serious, hard-working people, with a somewhat stoic manner.

Estonians are a people whose desire for self-determination runs deep. Perhaps this is why, after regaining independence in 1991, they were so quick to dust off a half-century of Soviet grey and rapidly catch up – economically and culturally – with the rest of Europe. Signs of the economic boom the country experienced after joining the European Union in 2004 are clearly visible in the shopping malls and high-rise hotels that dot the downtown area. However, that boom has long since tapered off. It was not enough to prevent an outflow of construction workers and medical staff seeking higher wages in Finland – an issue that continues to trouble the economy. On the more positive side of Estonia's recent growth is its transformation into an 'e-society', where the locals' love of all things high-tech has enabled a huge array of online government services and commercial apps. This is the city where Skype was born in 2003, where a citywide wi-fi network was rolled out more than fifteen years ago and where trials of a high-tech delivery robot named Starship were kick-started in 2017. In 2018, Estonia became one of the first nations with 5G network capability.

A SEASONAL CITY

Tallinn's extreme climate means it is a highly seasonal city as far as tourism – or anything else – goes. During the short period of warm weather, usually May to August, flocks of cruise-ship passengers

The candy-coloured houses lining Pikk jalg ('Long Leg' Street)

SUSTAINABLE TRAVEL

Few cities are as sustainable as Tallinn, whose post-Soviet success is underpinned by electronic transport, a revitalised urban centre and new cycle routes like the Reidi Road, which connects the ferry port to the rewilded coastline of Pirita. Awarded European Green Capital for 2023, Tallinn brought in ubiquitous water-filling fountains and new Green Key hotels – like the super-efficient *Schlössle* (Pühavaimu 13–15; www.schlosslehotel.com) in the medieval Old Town. Proactive visitors can take part in the annual Spring Clean-up Campaign in April/May with a stint planting trees, de-littering the beach or cleaning salt from the streets. Be sure to eat at one of a new guard of vegetarian and vegan restaurants; try the 'In Bloom' tasting menu at the zero-waste Michelin Green star-awarded restaurant in Fotografiska Tallinn (see page 79). Adventurers might like to take part in Estonia's new 'bikepacking' trend – heading beyond town to the beachy neighbourhoods of Paljassaare or Viimsi on a City Bike (www.citybike.ee) or an e-bike from the Bolt app (www.bolt.eu/en/ebikes). And if you want to explore further afield, Rail Baltica, the much-vaunted high-speed rail link set to connect Baltic capitals Tallinn Riga and Vilnius, is due to start up around 2030, making travel between Estonia, Lithuania and Latvia more sustainable.

and short-term visitors descend on the Old Town, filling the restaurants and hotel rooms. Still, summer is the best time to visit, when the weather is at its most inviting, festivals and concerts are easy to find, and the city is generally vibrant.

That said, a visit in the off-season is perfectly reasonable for anyone seeking to avoid crowds. There will still be plenty to see and do, even when outdoor cafés are no longer an option, and visitors will have the enchanting medieval streets almost to themselves. A visit during winter, provided you are wrapped up warm, can be a magical experience as snow blankets the tiled rooftops and the town turns on its Christmas charm.

10 Things not to miss

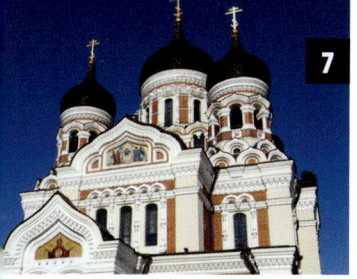

1 TOOMPEA CASTLE
This pretty pink palace has been the seat of power in Estonia since the thirteenth century. See page 37

2 DOME CHURCH
Turbulent history and a spectacular steeple characterise Tallinn's grand St Mary's cathedral. See page 42

3 TOOMPEA'S VIEWING PLATFORMS
Enjoy a fairy-tale panorama from these lofty viewpoints. See page 43

4 THE TOWN HALL
Fine medieval woodcarvings are among the Gothic building's treasures. See page 48

5 HOLY SPIRIT CHURCH
Its eye-catching clock has been ticking since the 1600s. See page 51

6 SEAPLANE HARBOUR
Explore historic ships in this vast maritime museum. See page 69

7 ALEXANDER NEVSKY CATHEDRAL
The legacy of Russia's Tsarist Empire is crowned by five impressive onion domes. See page 36

8 KUMU
The soul of the nation comes to light at Tallinn's grandest art museum. See page 72

9 TOWN HALL SQUARE
Tallinn's former central market is still the life and soul of the Old Town. See page 47

10 KADRIORG ART MUSEUM
Peter the Great's summer residence is a throwback to imperial Russia. See page 71

A perfect day in Tallinn

9AM

Breakfast. Get your energy fix with a breakfast of sausages and herring in your hotel, or grab a coffee and pastry in the Town Hall's medieval-style corner café. On Town Hall Square, find the polished stone representing the Centre of Tallinn and see how far you have to stretch to spot the five towers. See page 50.

9.30AM

St Nicholas viewpoint. Take the glass lift up the tower of St Nicholas Church for unrivalled views of medieval Tallinn and the bay. Pick out Aleksander Nevsky Cathedral's onion domes in the morning light. See page 62.

10.30AM

Old Town. Wander through the cobblestone streets and see how many colourful doorways you can find. For deeper historic insights, stop in at the Great Guild Hall (see page 54) or the Tallinn City Museum (see page 60).

12.30PM

Shopping. Head to St Catherine's Passage and wind through the craft workshops to watch artisans at work. Pore over the wares at Sweater Wall to find an authentic souvenir. If you're hungry, book a table at *Rado* (see page 117).

2PM

Kadriorg. Catch tram No. 1 to Kadriorg Park (see page 70), stroll around the leafy pathways and inspect the manicured flowerbeds behind Kadriorg Palace. Time permitting, take the path to the Russalka Memorial (see page 74) and gaze out over Tallinn Bay.

3.30PM

Culture fix. Connect to your creative side by visiting the art museums in Kadriorg. Aside from the award-winning modern art gallery Kumu (see page 72), the Mikkel Museum is worth a visit for its exquisite porcelain (see page 72). The palace itself shelters a vast collection of foreign art (see page 72).

6PM

Historic dining. Make your way back towards the Old Town by tram. Quell hunger pangs at the famed medieval-era restaurant *Olde Hansa* or its equally lively neighbour *Peppersack*; both built into charming Hanseatic houses. See page 117.

8PM

Bar-hopping. After dark, the bar terraces of the Old Town begin to fill with revellers. The basement bar *Karja Kelder* (Väike Karja 1) is a good place to sample Estonian beers, while *Nimeta* (Suur-Karja 4) is a guaranteed party spot with an international crowd. See page 94.

11PM

Dancing. If you're not ready to call it a night, crank it up a few gears with some live music (see page 96); try *Moku* at Telliskivi 57.

Tallinn on a budget

9.30AM

Morning stroll. Order a famous flat white and cinnamon bun from *Kiosk No.1* (Toompuiestee 22a) and strike out for the ancient city. Cut through the Danish King's Garden and look out for the Danish crest mounted on the stone ramparts, vestiges from the days of thirteenth-century King Waldemar II, who presided over the capture of the city by the Danes. See page 41.

11AM

Orient yourself. Meet at Niguliste 2 for a free guided walk in the old city through EstAdventures (www.estadventures.ee), a community-owned group of local storytellers. The Tallinn in a Nutshell tour covers medieval Toompea, Soviet influences and modern boom times. Groups of up to five people; book ahead for a €1 fee (tips of up to €5 are appreciated).

1PM

Lunch like a local. Stuff yourself over lunch at *Kompressor* (see page 116), a legendary pancake house that never skimps on its savoury ham-and-cheese — or pizza-like pepperoni and mozzarella — crêpes. With a house-special rhubarb lemonade, it comes in at just over €10. Even cheaper if you refill your water bottle at the station nearby at Nunne 18.

3PM

Pay your respects. Stroll over to Dome Church after the daily mass. For a €2 entrance fee, you can bask in a beam of afternoon light and marvel at the elaborate coat-of-arms collection. A hundred finely detailed 'epitaphs' hang on the white walls, honouring Estonian dignitaries buried underfoot. See page 42.

4.30PM

Refuel. When in Tallinn…grab a teatime pick-me-up at this classic Sõõrikukohvik doughnut shop (Kentmanni 21), one of two remaining in town. Fried, sugared doughnuts are sold by the kilo here, but singles are less than a euro. To reach this outpost, hop on a No. 3 bus at the Adamsoni stop, just outside the city walls, or find an e-bike through the Bolt app.

7.30PM

Catch the sunset. Tallinn's mammoth concrete amphitheatre, or Linnahall, was built by the Soviets for the Moscow Olympics — and looks like a Mayan pyramid reimagined in mid-century Europe. That doesn't mean it's not popular. Tallinners perch on the old stands and watch the sun sink into the Gulf of Finland. See page 70.

9PM

Have a brewski. On weekends, the craft beer shop and café *Brewklyn* stays open past sunset, so you can pick up a sassy-named American brew from the hundreds in store and take it out or crack it open on site. This Port Noblessner outfit often fires up the barbecue too. See page 95.

Family-friendly Tallinn

9AM
Grab breakfast. The three-storey Balti Jaam market doesn't care if you want chips, bubble tea, Uzbek dumplings or tiny pancakes for breakfast – all vendors open at 9am, and the tall, echoing atrium absorbs the sound of tiny yelps. See page 79.

10AM
Walk to the dock. Stroll fifteen minutes through Kalamaja, a genteel heritage neighbourhood studded with pretty timber houses. You'll emerge at the waterfront, site of a spooky former prison, the coast guard, an old submarine and a boat ramp. Follow the coastline around the working shipyard to the giant boat propeller propped up by the water's edge. See page 69.

10.30AM
Naval-gaze. Enter an actual submarine at the Seaplane Harbour. After examining the switches, levers and hatches, kids can explore the rest of the hangar-like space – it's incredibly interactive, with simulators, dress-up booths, a faux sea pitted with mines to avoid, and a themed playground. See page 69.

NOON
Supersize your lunch. The meal deals at the chicken joint *KotKot* look like fast food but the nuggets are fried fresh and the burgers are bigger than they have any right to be. Vegetarian options are almost indiscernible from their meaty alternatives. Sit outside by the marina or bag a 'snackbox' to go. See page 121.

1PM
Get hands-on. Look for the dinosaur statue outside Peetri 10 – it marks the entrance to PROTO, a virtual-reality museum in a cavernous hall displaying industrial-age inventions with steampunk allure. See page 69.

3PM
Enjoy the panorama. Find the stop behind PROTO and take the No. 73 bus to Freedom Square. From here it's a five-minute walk through the Old Town to the Niguliste Museum and its new glass lift, which takes visitors up the medieval church tower to a sky deck with 360-degree views of the city. See page 63.

4PM
Beach time. If the weather's kind, hop on a No. 8 bus to Pirita, to walk the forested trail to its long, pristine beach. Frolic in the sand, then order a budget dinner at *St Patrick's* (Supluse 1). Some families sit alfresco while the kids dip their toes in the surf.

6PM
Watch the sunset. There's still time to catch the last lift up the TV Tower, a quick ride from Pirita by bus or taxi. The 21st-floor open platform is the tallest in Northern Europe at 170m high, with views on a clear day to Finland. See page 77.

History

A quick glance at Tallinn's history will leave no doubt as to why locals are so passionate about their independence. For nearly the entire past eight centuries their nation has been ruled by foreign powers, starting with subjugation by the Danish crown, then German crusaders, the Polish-Lithuanian Commonwealth, the Swedish Empire, the Russian Empire and, most recently, the Soviet Union. It is remarkable that, against these odds, Estonians have been able to hang on to their language and cultural identity through the years.

The secret to their resilience might be that their roots run incredibly deep. While historians argue about exactly when the ancestors

Alexander Nevsky Cathedral on Toompea

of the ancient Eesti (or Aestii, as the Romans may have called them) arrived on the Baltic coast, most put the date some time between 8000 and 3000BC.

Little is known about the pre-Christian period of Estonia's history, but archaeological evidence suggests that in the years before the arrival of the first invaders, the northern Rävala people lived a clan-like existence, engaged in farming, fishing and, increasingly, trade with their Baltic Sea neighbours. By the twelfth century AD, they had built a wooden fortress on Toompea Hill, which Arab cartographer Abu Abdallah Muhammad al-Idrisi marked on his world map in 1154 as a 'seasonal stronghold'. This was the first mention of Tallinn in historical records.

Danish knights battle local pagans in 1219

FIRST INVADERS

In the early thirteenth century, the Pope's call for a crusade against pagans around the Baltic Sea prompted a bloody and complicated struggle between Swedes, Danes, Russians, German crusaders and local tribes. As part of this land grab, King Valdemar II of Denmark conquered the Estonians' stronghold on Toompea in 1219, immediately replacing it with his own fortress. Valdemar's victory marked the beginning of a long period of foreign rule, with Toompea, the hill at Tallinn's centre, the regional seat of power.

Meanwhile, German crusaders battled their way northward from their foothold in Riga. In 1227, they occupied Toompea and gained control of the Danish holdings. German merchant families were invited to settle at the foot of Toompea Hill, sowing the seeds of a commercial capital. For the next seven hundred years, the descendants of these 'Baltic Germans' remained the dominant class in the city.

A CITY BUILT ON SALT

Tallinn's heyday came between the thirteenth and sixteenth centuries, when it flourished as a major trading port on the route between East and West. Its development into a booming merchant centre kicked off in 1248, when the Danish king allowed Tallinn to adopt the Lübeck law, effectively making it a self-ruling city state.

Seventeenth-century Tallinn

What's more, around 1284 Tallinn became a member of the Hanseatic League, a powerful association of cities that held a monopoly over northern European trade.

As the key Hansa port dealing with trade to Russia, Tallinn was guaranteed success. Russian fur and wax and Estonian grain and linen were exported to cities in Western Europe, while textiles, herring, wine and spices were shuttled in the opposite direction. The most valuable commodity that came through Tallinn, however, was salt, said to be worth its weight in gold at the time. In fact, so much profitable saline cargo changed hands here on its way east that Tallinn became known as a 'city built on salt'.

It was during the boom years of the 1300s and 1400s that most of the present-day Old Town took shape. The city wall and towers were built and improved, workshops sprung up and a new Town Hall was installed in 1404 to house the City Council, the powerful body controlling town life and international trade.

In 1346, Toompea's tenants changed. Denmark, then having its own internal difficulties, sold northern Estonia to the Riga-based German knights. Thus all of Estonia came under the control of the Livonian Order, which already ruled southern Estonia and present-day Latvia. In independent Tallinn, however, the political shake-up had little impact.

> **NOTES**
>
> 'We shall never be great in number or strength, therefore we must become great in spirit' – pastor and linguist Jakob Hurt, a key figure in Estonia's National Awakening.

FROM EMPIRE TO EMPIRE

Fortunes shifted drastically in the mid-sixteenth century with the outbreak of the Livonian War (1558–83). By now the Livonian state was in decline. Smelling blood, Russia, Sweden, Denmark and the Polish-Lithuanian Commonwealth all moved in for a share of the Baltic stakes. Tallinn and the nobles on Toompea negotiated surrender with Sweden in 1561, but the war would rage on for two more decades.

The Swedish Period of the nation's history was characterised by enlightened social policies, including more rights for peasants and the establishment of an education system. But the city itself deteriorated. Post-war plagues and famines caused Tallinn's population to plummet, and its role as a trade gateway to Russia was overtaken by competitors. The boom times were clearly over.

Conflict broke out again in the early eighteenth century, this time with imperial Sweden and an expansionist Russia fighting over Baltic territories in the devastating Great Northern War (1700–21). In 1710 Tsar Peter the Great captured Tallinn from the Swedes, and Estonia became a province of the Russian Empire. Estonian peasants lost the privileges they'd gained under Swedish rule and were forced into slave-like serfdom.

NATIONAL AWAKENING

The nineteenth century, by contrast, brought huge improvements for ethnic Estonians. Serfdom was abolished in 1816, and from 1860 to 1880 a cultural revival referred to as the National Awakening reached its height. Societies of 'Estophiles' promoted Estonian literature and culture, previously considered of little value. Estonian poetry bloomed, Estonian-language newspapers appeared and the national epic *Kalevipoeg* was compiled. The nation previously seen as country folk started proudly calling themselves Estonians.

Estonian War of Independence

At the same time, key political and demographic changes were afoot. Completion of the St Petersburg–Tallinn railway line in 1870 brought a wave of industrial growth to Tallinn, and with it thousands of ethnic Estonian and Russian factory workers.

THE MANY NAMES OF TALLINN

Tallinn's oldest recorded name is Qaleveni, as Arab cartographer al-Idrisi marked on his world map in 1154. Old Russian chronicles used the somewhat similar Kolyvan, while Scandinavians probably referred to the city as Lindanise or Lindana. From the Middle Ages until the early twentieth century, the ruling ethnic German elite used the name Reval (or Rewel), as the city was at the centre of ancient Rävala.

Estonians, however, called it Tallinn. The name originates from Danish rule (1219–1346) when the city was referred to as *Castrum Danorum* (Danish Castle), which in Estonian was *tannin lidna*. Another theory is that Tallinn comes from a fusion of *Taani* (Danish) and *linn* (city), which first became Taanilinna and later Tallinn. After independence in 1918, the capital's official name was changed from Reval to Tallinn.

Germans were now outnumbered in the city, and in 1904 they lost municipal elections to an Estonian-Russian bloc. For the first time, non-Germans controlled Tallinn.

THE ESTONIAN REPUBLIC

On 24 February 1918, with the imperial Russian government ousted and World War I raging, Estonia declared independence. Before the new Estonian Republic could become a reality, it would undergo months of German occupation, then fight a War of Independence against the Bolsheviks. But by 1920, the Estonians finally had their own state.

Life in the fledgling republic was far from perfect. The economic situation remained poor through the 1930s, and divisions between right-wing and left-wing extremists deepened. In 1934, the head of state (and later president) Konstantin Päts led a military coup to keep ultra-nationalists from power. Though Päts stifled democracy and brought the country to near authoritarian rule, he remained a popular figure.

A Nazi recruitment poster in 1942

In the late 1930s, a long-awaited economic turnaround fuelled a building boom in Tallinn, and the republic's future looked bright.

WORLD WAR II AND OCCUPATION

World War II brought an end to the new country's aspirations. The Soviets occupied Estonia in June 1940, and absorbed it into the USSR. A brutal year of arrests, executions and mass deportations to Siberian prison camps ensued. Unsurprisingly, when the Nazis drove out the Soviets in 1941, the Estonians at first saw them as liberators. But their euphoria died after it became clear that the Germans wouldn't restore independence but rather impose their own harsh policies. During the three-year Nazi occupation, many Estonians were co-opted into the German Army while others joined voluntarily, seeing it as their best chance to stave off another Soviet invasion.

When that annexation came in September 1944, thousands of Estonians fled in boats to Sweden, establishing a strong émigré community that kept the culture alive in exile. Around 30,000 to 35,000 others, known as the Forest Brothers, hid deep in Estonia's woods and started a ten-year campaign of resistance. The worst fears about renewed Soviet atrocities came to pass. After the war, 36,000 people were arrested and accused of aiding the Nazis, and over the next years, countless families were loaded onto cattle cars and sent to Siberia.

Conditions normalised somewhat in the post-Stalin 1950s. Industries grew and hundreds of thousands of ethnic Russians were relocated to Estonia, both to work in factories and to Russify the Soviet territory. Over the next decades, life was generally as stifled as it was in the rest of the USSR, but in many ways the situation in Estonia was better than elsewhere – shops were better stocked and Finnish TV broadcasts provided a window to the West.

THE SINGING REVOLUTION

The seeds of Estonia's independence movement were sown during the *perestroika* years of 1987 and 1988 with the first large-scale demonstrations against the Soviet regime. Mass singing events held in June 1988 saw more than 100,000 people packing Tallinn's Song Festival Grounds for successive nights. These protests stirred a new national awakening and gave the movement its name, the Singing Revolution.

On 20 August 1991 the Supreme Soviet of the Republic of Estonia declared the nation's independence. Statues of Lenin were immediately tore down, and countries around the world, including the USSR, recognised Estonia's statehood. The Republic of Estonia was restored.

BOOM TIMES, SKYPE AND BEYOND

When independence was re-established, Estonia found itself facing a wrecked economy, a tense relationship with its eastern neighbour and a Russian-speaking minority unsure of its role in the new republic. The latter two issues came to the fore in April 2007, when the government's attempts to relocate a Red Army monument from the centre of Tallinn sparked two nights of rioting by ethnic Russian youths.

For the most part, however, the latest chapter of the nation's history has been marked by healing and reintegration with the West. A brief period of 'cowboy capitalism' in the 1990s gave way to an investment and tourism boom that transformed the Tallinn skyline and boosted national pride, particularly once Estonia joined the EU in 2004. Meanwhile, tech-savvy locals were busy building the country's reputation as a hotbed of software innovation, with Skype becoming the nation's best-known export. The term 'e-Estonia' is now widely used to describe both the country and this phenomenon.

The fast-paced growth between 2005 and 2007 was brought to a grinding halt by the worldwide economic crisis. Estonia weathered the storm with tough fiscal belt-tightening, eventually joining the Eurozone in 2011 – a risky but significant step in establishing itself as a player on the world stage. Recently, the country has marked its anniversary of independence (24 February) under the shadow of Russia's invasion of Ukraine.

CHRONOLOGY

1154 Tallinn is marked on Arab cartographer al-Idrisi's world map.
1219 King Valdemar II of Denmark conquers northern Estonia.
1227–38 Riga-based German crusaders wrest control of Tallinn and northern Estonia from the Danes; German merchants settle in Tallinn.
1248 Tallinn adopts the Lübeck law to become a self-governing trade city.
1284 Tallinn becomes a member of the Hanseatic League.
1346 Danes sell their Estonian holdings to German knights in Riga, putting Estonia under the rule of the Livonian Order.

1558–83 The Livonian War between Russia, Poland, Sweden and Denmark leaves Estonia under Swedish rule.
1684 A massive fire devastates Toompea.
1710 During the Great Northern War (1700–21), Sweden loses Estonia to the Russian Empire.
1816 Serfdom is abolished.
1860–80 National Awakening.
1870 The St Petersburg–Tallinn rail connection is completed.
1918 Estonia declares independence.
1940 Soviets invade, forcibly annexing Estonia to the USSR.
1941–44 Nazi invasion and occupation.
1944 Soviet forces reinvade. Almost 50 years of occupation follows.
1987–88 The Singing Revolution.
1991 Estonia regains independence.
2004 Estonia joins NATO and the European Union.
2011 Estonia adopts the euro.
2017 Eight hundred British troops are deployed in Estonia as a deterrent to potential Russian aggression.
2021 Kaja Kallas became Estonia's first woman prime minister.
2022 Russia invades Ukraine. Estonia aids Ukraine.
2024 Estonia's parliament votes in Kristen Michal as prime minister in July after Kallas resigns to take up the post of the European Union's chief diplomat.

Estonia joined the EU in 2004

The distinctive onion domes of Alexander Nevsky Cathedral

Places

When arriving in Tallinn, most visitors' first instinct is to head straight into the Old Town – and rightly so. This tightly packed ensemble of winding, cobblestone streets, beautiful medieval dwellings, breathtaking church spires, café-filled squares and half-hidden courtyards isn't just Tallinn's biggest tourist draw, it's also the heart and soul of the city. Better still, it's all neatly packaged within a centuries-old town wall, giving it a fairy-tale charm and at the same time making it easy to navigate and explore.

For a complete picture of the city, however, it is also essential to venture beyond the medieval centre to see the wooden houses and offbeat attractions of bohemian Kalamaja, the art and extravagance of Kadriorg and other surprising finds awaiting in the outlying areas.

Our tour starts at the birthplace of Tallinn: Old Town. Today this district seems like one big medieval mosaic, but it is actually made up of what were historically two distinct entities – Toompea Hill, home of the gentry and the representatives of Estonia's ruling power, and Lower Town, an autonomous Hanseatic trading city populated by merchants and craftspeople.

TOOMPEA

HIGHLIGHTS
- Pikk Jalg and Lühike Jalg, see page 35
- Orthodox Cathedral, see page 36
- Toompea Castle, see page 37
- Kiek in de Kök and Bastion Tunnels, see page 39
- Danish King's Garden, see page 41
- Dome Church, see page 42
- Kohtuotsa viewing platform, see page 43

The cobblestoned Pikk jalg

Take one look down from the edge of this 24m (78ft) limestone hill and you will understand why Toompea has always been synonymous with power. Not only did its steep slopes provide a natural defence against would-be invaders, the high elevation offered a commanding view of the comings and goings in the harbour nearby. It is no wonder, then, that ancient Estonians picked this spot to build a wooden stronghold, now thought to be the kernel of Tallinn. That fortress is long gone, but the tradition it started has continued. From the Danes in 1219 to the Russians in the early twentieth century, every foreign empire that ruled the northern Estonian lands has used Toompea as its power base, stationing its political representatives in Toompea Castle.

The fortified area outside the castle, meanwhile, was home to Estonia's gentry. German landlords, owners of feudal estates in the surrounding countryside, built grand, often palatial houses on Toompea from where they would look down, both literally and figuratively, on the busy merchants and workers in Lower Town. Today most of these houses are embassies, government offices or high-priced flats.

Given Toompea's history as the seat of the ruling power, it is somehow fitting that both Estonia's Parliament and its government administration are now located here. What draws tourists to Toompea isn't these grand institutions, though. It's the prospect of seeing two of the nation's most spectacular churches and taking in the best views of Tallinn.

PIKK JALG AND LÜHIKE JALG

Four roads and four stairways lead up to Toompea, but by far the most interesting paths up the hill are Tallinn's two 'legs' – **Pikk jalg** ('Long Leg' Street) and **Lühike jalg** ('Short Leg' Street).

In medieval times, if you were travelling by horse or carriage, you would have taken Pikk jalg to reach Toompea from Lower Town. It starts at the end of Pikk Street at the curious-looking **Long Leg Gate Tower** ❶ (Pika jala väravatorn) and continues in a straight, steady climb to **Castle Square** (Lossi plats). The four-sided gate tower was built in 1380, but its present shape comes from a mid-fifteenth-century reconstruction. Pikk jalg itself is a favourite haunt of local artists vying to sell their works to passersby. High above the creatives' heads, the extravagant mansions strung along the cliff edge nod to the wealth and power of Toompea's gentry.

> **NOTES**
>
> Pikk jalg is so steep that anyone driving a carriage down it was in for a harrowing experience, according to nineteenth-century accounts. Before the carriage started off, coachmen and tower guards had to shout to one another to ensure the area at the bottom was clear of traffic.

St Nicholas Church

Picturesque Lühike jalg was historically the main pedestrian passage into Toompea. Though officially a street, it is really just a narrow, winding lane with a staircase. Today it is flanked by some of Tallinn's more intriguing art shops, and is also home to the **Adamson-Eric Museum** (https://adamson-eric.ekm.ee/en; charge), which showcases the works of Adamson Eric (1902–68), one of the most outstanding Estonian painters and applied artists of the twentieth century. At the top of the street's 16m (52ft) climb stands the 1456-built **Short Leg Gate Tower** ❷ (Lühikese jala väravatorn). The sturdy wooden door you pass here is the original dating from the seventeenth century.

ORTHODOX CATHEDRAL

When you reach Castle Square at the top of Toompea, you come to a dramatic, onion-domed church that looks straight out of a Russian film. This is the **Alexander Nevsky Cathedral** ❸ (www.cathedral.bg; free), the most imposing Orthodox church in Estonia and an important place of worship for Tallinn's Orthodox faithful. Built from 1894 to 1900, the cathedral is a relatively new addition to Toompea. It was designed by St Petersburg architect Mikhail Preobrazhensky and follows the same basic layout as the five-domed churches that appeared in Moscow and Jaroslavl in the seventeenth century.

Though the cathedral serves a purely spiritual purpose these days, it was originally placed here as a blatant symbol of Russian power. In the late nineteenth century, imperial Russia was carrying out an intense campaign of Russification in its outer provinces. As part of its drive to assert cultural dominance over the mainly Lutheran Germans and Estonians, the tsarist government built this towering Orthodox cathedral directly in front of the castle, on what had been one of the city's most famous squares.

A chance to see the cathedral's interior shouldn't be passed up. Visitors are welcome to enter and view the awe-inspiring **icons**, mosaics and other works of religious art that line the walls. The cathedral also operates a small gift shop to the right of the entrance.

TOOMPEA CASTLE

Next to the cathedral stands a large pink edifice that bears a distinctly regal look. This is the front of **Toompea Castle** ❹ (Toompea Loss), historic seat of power in Estonia and home to the Riigikogu, Estonia's parliament. The castle's origins date to

KALEV'S GRAVE

According to legend, Toompea is actually the burial mound of Kalev, the mythical figure who founded Tallinn. When Kalev died, his grief-stricken widow Linda started to cover his grave with stone after stone, and the distraught woman kept at it until she had created this bulging hill.

During the construction of the Alexander Nevsky Cathedral, a rumour surfaced that workers digging the space for the foundations had stumbled onto Kalev's grave. They supposedly uncovered an iron door bearing the inscription 'Cursed be anyone who dares disturb my peace'. As building continued, cracks began to appear in the cathedral's foundations. People took this as a sign of impending doom – either for the cathedral or for Tallinn as a whole. Luckily, the much-feared disaster never came to pass.

Tall Hermann tower and the Parliament Building at Governor's Gardens

1227–29, when the Knights of the Sword replaced the wooden stronghold that pagan Estonians had used to defend the hill with their own square fortress, which they surrounded with a circular stone wall. In the fourteenth century this was rebuilt into a convent-style fortress with a trapezoidal inner courtyard, 20m (65ft) walls and four corner towers, three of which are still standing. The **Baroque palace** you see in front of you was built from 1767 to 1773 on the order of Russian Empress Catherine the Great, and served as the administration building for the Russian provincial government in Estonia during tsarist times. The three-storey **Parliament Building** (www.riigikogu.ee; free; prebooking and valid photo ID are essential) in the courtyard, not visible from the outside, was built in the Expressionist style between 1920 and 1922 on the foundations of the former convent.

The **Governor's Garden** to the left of the castle is the best place to view another Tallinn landmark, **Tall Hermann** (Pikk Hermann). The tower was built onto the corner of the castle in 1371, but only reached its final 46m (150ft) height after reconstruction in 1500. Tradition dictates that whichever nation flies its flag on Tall Hermann rules Estonia.

On 24 February 1989, in what was one of the boldest gestures of Estonia's push for independence from the USSR, the Estonian blue, black and white flag was raised here in place of the red Soviet one. Estonia's colours have flown on Tall Hermann every day since – a potent symbol of the nation's sovereignty.

To see the castle's medieval flank, detour down Falgi Street, south of the fortress. Then return to Toompea to discover more of the town's old defences.

Kiek in de Kök

KIEK IN DE KÖK AND BASTION TUNNELS

Follow the steps leading down from the south side of Alexander Nevsky Cathedral and continue through a small park. Here you'll see a large, round medieval tower that looks like it could withhold any amount of cannon fire. This is **Kiek in de Kök** ❺, the Baltic region's most powerful cannon tower. Its name, which in Low German literally means 'peek into the kitchen', refers to the edifice's 36m (118ft) height. Soldiers posted here joked that they could see right down the chimneys and into the kitchens of the houses below.

Kiek in de Kök was built between 1475 and 1476 as a much smaller tower, and then almost immediately rebuilt to its current mammoth size. It was finally put to the test during the Livonian War (1558–83) when Ivan the Terrible's forces besieged Tallinn twice, once blowing a hole in its top floor large enough 'to drive two oxen through', according to historic accounts.

Now the tower operates as an extensive, modern **museum** (http://linnamuuseum.ee/en/kiek-de-kok; charge) chronicling the development of the town and its defences from the thirteenth to the eighteenth century. Apart from examining the antique weaponry and other displays, a visit here will allow you to climb the old staircases that run through the tower's 4m (13ft) -thick walls and take in the dizzying view from the top floor.

The Dome Church

The museum is also the gateway to the **Bastion Tunnels**, the once-secret defence system that runs beneath this edge of Toompea. Originally built in the late 1600s to ferry powder and soldiers, the tunnels found new life in the twentieth century as a bomb shelter. A visit requires signing up for a group tour in advance. Enquire at the ticket desk or phone ahead (tel: 644 6686).

Old towers and ramparts around the Danish King's Garden

The tour incorporates an informational film and may include a 'train ride' towards the Swedish bastion, or a visit to the adjoining Carved Sone Museum.

DANISH KING'S GARDEN

On the way back to Castle Square you can take a good look at more towers by tracing the thick town wall on the right. Crossing through a rectangular passage in the wall near the church takes you to the **Danish King's Garden** ❻ (Taani kuninga aed), an open area at the top of Lühike jalg, from where a set of terraced steps leads down to Rüütli Street. According to legend, this is the birthplace of the Danish flag. King Valdemar II supposedly camped on this spot when his forces were first trying to conquer Toompea in 1219. The Danes had been losing the battle when suddenly, it is

> **NOTES**
>
> After Toompea burned in 1684, there was so much rubble in the area that the ground level was raised by more than a metre. Because workers used the original floor when rebuilding Dome Church, anyone now entering the church has to take several steps down from street level.

said, the skies opened up and a red flag with a white cross floated downwards from the heavens. Spurred on by this miraculous sign, the Danes were able to fight onwards to victory. The two towers here – the small, round **Stable Tower** (Tallitorn) and the larger, square **Maiden's Tower** (Neitsitorn) – both date from the fourteenth century. The name 'Maiden's Tower' is an exercise in medieval irony: the building was actually a prison for sex workers.

DOME CHURCH

Both Toom-Kooli Street and Piiskopi Street lead from Castle Square to **Church Square** (Kiriku plats), home to the majestic-looking **Dome Church** ❼ (Toomkirik; http://toomkirik.ee; donation required), which is the headquarters of the Lutheran church of Estonia. Officially called the **Cathedral of St Mary the Virgin**, it was probably established not long after the Danes arrived in Toompea in 1219. Records first mention the church in 1233, by which time Dominican monks had already replaced the original wooden structure with one a stone construction. The church's vaulted main body is thought to originate from a fourteenth-century redesign.

In 1684 a devastating fire ripped through Toompea, destroying nearly every building, including the Dome Church. Though the church was operating again two years later, reconstruction work lasted until the end of the century. The **Baroque tower**, open to visitors in summer, was a later addition; it dates from 1778–79.

The most striking aspect of the church's interior is the huge collection of funeral **coats of arms** covering the walls. These intricate works of art, dating mostly from the seventeenth to the twentieth century, traditionally accompanied the casket during funeral processions and were later kept in the church as a memorial. Most reflect a Baroque style, as does the rest of the church's interior. The intricate **Baroque pulpit** and **high altar** were both carved by the Tallinn sculptor Christian Ackermann and completed in 1696.

Along the northern wall, opposite the entrance, are the lavish **tombs** of some fairly eminent historic figures. These include Pontus de la Gardie (died 1585), the French-born head of the Swedish forces during the Livonian War; AJ von Krusenstern (died 1848), a Baltic German explorer who was the first to circumnavigate the globe under the Russian flag; and Admiral Samuel Greig of Fife, Scotland (1735–88), commander of Russia's Baltic Fleet and reputed lover of Catherine the Great.

VIEWING PLATFORMS

Heading from the church down Kohtu Street will take you past some impressive eighteenth- and nineteenth-century houses once owned by Toompea's noble elite. The road ends at the **Kohtuotsa viewing platform** ❽, where you'll be rewarded by a spectacular view of the red-tiled roofs of

Tallinn's characteristic towers

THE TOWN WALL

Stone barricades were established around Tallinn as early as 1265, but the town wall's current shape comes from an extensive reconstruction undertaken in the fourteenth century. The wall was continually improved through the years and by the time of its sixteenth-century heyday, it was 2.4km (1.5 miles) long, 14–16m (46–52ft) high and up to 3m (10ft) thick, and had a total of 46 towers. Today, 1.9km (1.2 miles) of the wall are still standing, as are 20 defence towers, two inner gate towers, and sections of two outer gate towers.

The closest segment of the wall you see from the Patkuli viewing platform, connecting the **Nunna**, **Sauna** and **Kuldjala** towers, is open to tourists. A visit here is the best way to view Tallinn's defences up close and to enjoy wonderful views of Toompea. When downhill in Lower Town, follow your map to the corner of Gümnaasiumi and Suur-Kloostri and look for the entrance to the **Town Wall** (Linnamüür).

the medieval Old Town, as well as the modern-looking city beyond the ancient walls.

The roof with the cockerel-shaped weathervane in the immediate foreground belongs to the Long Leg Gate Tower, its fairy-tale look contrasting sharply with the contemporary skyline. The tall medieval church on the left towards the port is St Olav's Church; the one much closer and on the right is St Nicholas Church. Among the buildings in the centre of the Old Town, try to spot the two very similar towers of the Town Hall and the Holy Spirit Church.

Further in the distance, beyond the high-rise hotels and office blocks, you can glimpse the arched rim of the **Tallinn Song Festival Arena** and the triangle-shaped ruins of **St Bridget's Convent**. The spire on the horizon is the **Tallinn TV Tower** and the rows of giant apartment blocks to its right mark the suburb of Lasnamäe.

A slightly different view is on offer at the nearby **Patkuli viewing platform** ❾, which can be reached by turning right on

VIEWING PLATFORMS   45

Toom-Rüütli, then left at the end of that street onto a nearly hidden passage. This platform looks over the northern section of the Old Town and affords an excellent view, taking in St Olav's Church, the **town wall** and several of its **towers**.

The lavish manor house standing on the cliff immediately to the left of the platform is **Stenbock House** ❿ (Stenbocki maja; www.riigikantselei.ee). Built in the late eighteenth century, it has been a courthouse and, at one time, a private home. After years of Soviet-era dilapidation it was restored in the 1990s and is now the office of the Government of Estonia.

From the Patkuli viewing platform you can head straight down Rahukohtu Street to continue touring Toompea, or make your way down the Patkuli Steps and into Lower Town.

Patkuli viewing platform

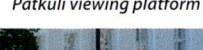

LOWER TOWN

HIGHLIGHTS

- » Town Hall Square, see page 47
- » Holy Spirit Church, see page 51
- » The Guilds of Pikk Street, see page 53
- » St Olav's Church, see page 57
- » The Great Coast Gate and around, see page 59
- » The Latin Quarter, see page 60
- » St Nicholas Church, see page 62
- » Freedom Square, see page 64

For most visitors, it is Lower Town (All-Linn) that defines Tallinn. This is where the crowds mingle, where bicycle taxis, Segway riders and almond-sellers jostle for space on the medieval streets, where tourists come to gaze at historic curiosities of every sort or simply to relax and take in the timeless atmosphere of the Old Town. In short, this is where life happens in Tallinn.

In that respect, little has changed since medieval times. The area we now call Lower Town was then the Hanseatic city of Tallinn (or Reval, as it was known at the time), a busy trading city of international stature. In 1248 it was granted autonomous status and from then on had its own government, local laws, social institutions and defence forces. More importantly, it was the domain of merchants and artisans, labourers and servants, all of whom would have contributed to the general bustle of commerce as they went about their daily lives.

Centuries of activity have left Lower Town with a wealth of fascinating sights, many of which are nicely complemented by the museums, cafés and other businesses among them.

TOWN HALL SQUARE

Through the centuries, the social and cultural heart of Tallinn has always been **Town Hall Square** ⓫ (Raekoja plats), the attractive open area at the centre of the Old Town. In medieval times it served as the town's main marketplace and was also the site of tournaments, festivals and at least one execution. Even now the

Cafés and market stalls in the attractive Town Hall Square

CRIME AND PUNISHMENT

In addition to the other functions it had in medieval times, Town Hall Square served as a place of public punishment. For example, women accused of gossiping were sentenced to walk around the square three times while enduring the whistling and jeering of the crowds. Look for the iron shackles mounted on one pillar of the Town Hall. These were used to punish people guilty of petty crimes such as swindling and non-payment of debts. In more serious cases, convicts would be locked in a pillory that once stood on the square.

The town also employed an executioner, but as a rule the executions took place on a hill outside the town. One notable exception occurred in the late seventeenth century. A drunken priest named Panicke ordered an omelette at an inn and, finding it 'hard as the sole of a shoe', sent it back. Upon being served two more such horrendous omelettes, he grabbed an axe and slaughtered the waitress. Once sober, the priest turned himself in, begging to be executed. So heinous was his crime that the sentence was carried out immediately, right on the square. Two long stones in the shape of an 'L', not far from the Town Hall Pharmacy, mark the place where he was beheaded, though the spot may be covered by café tables in summer.

---

square acts as the chief gathering place for the city's residents, each year hosting concerts, art markets and festival events. Town Hall Square is invariably packed with umbrella-shaded café terraces in spring and summer, and every winter it is home to an elaborate Christmas market centred around the town Christmas tree, a tradition dating back to at least 1441.

Presiding over the square is Tallinn's **Town Hall** (Raekoda; http://raekoda.tallinn.ee; charge). Historic records indicate that another town hall occupied this spot as early as 1322, but the late-Gothic structure you see today was completed in 1404. **Old Thomas** (Vana Toomas), the soldier-shaped weathervane perched atop the spire, has been watching over the city since 1530, while the

Baroque spire itself and the fanciful, dragon-shaped drainpipes both date from 1627.

Tallinn's powerful Town Council would hold meetings on the hall's main floor upstairs, where the beautiful, vaulted **Citizens' Hall** and **Council Chamber** are located. The wooden benches that occupy them are decorated with intricate medieval carvings that easily qualify as art treasures. The ground floor, by contrast, was more a place of business, encompassing a trading hall, treasury and counting room, while the basement housed a torture chamber. Unfortunately, the Town Hall is open to drop-in visitors only from late June through August, but visits can be arranged for other times of the year by appointment (tel: 6457 900; email tuuli.uustal@tallinnlv.ee). Anyone not afraid of heights should also climb the 64m (210ft) **Town Hall Tower** (Raekoja torn; charge), open June through August, for a great view of the Old Town.

An outdoor café on Town Hall Square

Tucked behind the Town Hall is the fifteenth-century **Town Hall Prison** (Raevangla), where those arrested were kept before trial. It now houses the interesting **Museum of Photography** (www.linnamuuseum.ee/en/museum-of-photography; charge) chronicling 150 years of photographic pursuits in the city and displaying various antique cameras. Some exhibits occupy the old cells downstairs.

Back on Town Hall Square you'll see thousands of stones covering the ground, but there is one of particular interest: a large, round slab decorated with a compass rose. You can find it by standing at the corner of the Town Hall, directly in front of the café, and following a seam in the pattern of bricks 25 or 30 paces out into the square. Tour guides call this stone the **Centre of Tallinn**, a name that isn't based so much on geography as it is on the fact that you can theoretically see the tops of all five of the Old Town's spires from here. Be prepared to stretch, bend and/or jump to achieve this goal.

In a corner of the square opposite the Town Hall stands the **Town Hall Pharmacy** (Raeapteek), one of the oldest continuously running pharmacies in Europe. Records first mention it in 1422, but it may have been established decades earlier. Amazingly, between 1580 and 1911 the pharmacy was managed by ten generations of the same family. Some of the useful preparations sold here

THE CAT'S WELL

Tallinn was not always the most animal-friendly place in times past. On the corner of Rataskaevu and Dunkri streets stands a picturesque covered wheel well, the subject of countless tourist snapshots. Few visitors, however, realise that the well has a highly unsavoury legend attached to it.

In medieval times, locals believed a water spirit lived in the well, and that it would become angry and flood the town unless residents gave it regular animal sacrifices. So all sorts of creatures – mostly dead, but some living – were thrown down the deep chasm. The main victims of this superstitious practice were stray felines, giving rise to the well's popular nickname, Cat's Well.

The practice did little to improve the quality of the water drawn from here, though in reality the problem may have had more to do with the water's high lime content. In either case, the well had fallen into disuse by the nineteenth century and was filled in.

in centuries past include minced bat, burnt bees, snakeskin and powdered unicorn horn. Everyday items such as paper, wax, gunpowder and claret were available as well. A dubious local legend insists that marzipan was invented on the site.

These days you'll find the same remedies here as in any modern pharmacy, but in homage to its history, the location maintains a small **exhibition room** (www.raeapteek.ee; free), displaying antique equipment, archaic medicines and similar artefacts.

A colourful town house beside the Church of the Holy Spirit

HOLY SPIRIT CHURCH

Just a few paces north of Town Hall Square through Saiakang passage stands a radiant white church with an octagonal tower. This is the **Holy Spirit Church** ⑫ (Püha Vaimu kirik; charge), tiny in comparison to the Old Town's other medieval churches, but enormous in the hearts of ordinary Estonians for the role it played in their cultural history. It was here that the very first sermons were given in the Estonian language after the Reformation. And in 1535 the church's pastor, Johann Koell, translated and published what is thought to be the first book in Estonian. Balthasar Russow, one of the most important chroniclers of the Livonian period, was pastor here from 1566 until his death in 1600.

Keeping time at the Holy Spirit Church

The church was important to Tallinn's medieval administration as well: it served as a chapel for the Town Council, and one of its rooms was used for signing contracts and treaties, the sanctity of the church ensuring the subsequent honesty of all parties. Mostly, however, this was a church for the common folk. As early as the thirteenth century it operated an almshouse tending to the city's sick, elderly and poor and, in contrast to other churches, the Holy Spirit Church's congregation was made up of Tallinn's lower class.

The building was completed in the 1360s and its overall shape dates from that period. Its **Baroque spire**, however, is a newer installation; it was added after a major fire in 1684 destroyed its Renaissance-style predecessor. The most eye-catching addition to the church is the large blue-and-gold **clock** on the facade near the main doorway. Created by Tallinn's best-known woodcarver,

Christian Ackermann, in the late seventeenth century, this is the city's oldest – and by far its most captivating – public timepiece. The figures you see in each of its corners represent the four gospels.

As attractive as both the spire and clock are, the church's most impressive feature is unquestionably its rich interior. Decorated from almost floor to ceiling with lavishly carved woodwork, including Baroque pews and a Renaissance pulpit, the ensemble is truly awe-inspiring. The church's best-loved piece is the **altar**, commissioned from the renowned Lübeck sculptor and painter Bernt Notke in 1483. Figures of the Virgin Mary with child, apostles and saints, all painted in bright, clear blue, red and gold, stand at the centre of the cupboard-type altarpiece.

THE GUILDS OF PIKK STREET

Leading from the area just north of Town Hall Square to the northernmost tip of the Old Town is the aptly named Pikk Street, or 'Long Street'. It was the longest street in medieval Tallinn, a busy artery connecting the port to the town's main marketplace. Not only was it the principal route for merchants visiting the city, it was also home to several guild associations.

From the fourteenth century these guilds, all-important associations of merchants and craftspeople, played a major role in town politics and society. Though many took on the character of religious brotherhoods,

> **NOTES**
>
> The city's oldest café, **Maiasmokk** (Sweet tooth; www.kohvikmaiasmokk.ee/en), has been selling cakes and pastries from the same spot at Pikk 16 since 1864. Guests can sip coffee while basking in its early-twentieth-century ambience. A separate entrance around the corner leads into the **Kalev Marzipan Museum Room** (www.kalev.eu; free), where hundreds of elaborate marzipan figurines are on display.

they were actually profession-based organisations that acted as both trade unions and the architects of Tallinn's social life, arranging weddings, feasts and public celebrations.

The grand looking building at Pikk 17, just across from the Holy Spirit Church, is the **Great Guild Hall** ⓭ (Suurgildi hoone), which served as a meeting place for Tallinn's Great Guild, a group of wealthy merchants who wielded considerable influence over town affairs. The hall was completed around 1410 and has changed little since that time. The red and white symbols on its facade represent the guild's coat of arms, and the fanciful lion's-head doorknockers date from 1430. The hall is now home to the **Estonian History Museum** (www.ajaloomuuseum.ee; charge), which presents a high-tech, engaging overview of 11,000 years of the nation's development. The

Estonian History Museum

exhibition in the cellar provides insight into the building itself and how it was used through the years, while paving slabs in Börsi kaik lane outside each have a historic event marked on them, forming a timeline of Estonia's past (with a few references to its possible future).

Further north along Pikk, on the right-hand side, you'll see the eccentric facade of the **Draakon Gallery**, (www.eaa.ee/draakon), adorned with carved seahorse-tailed serpents and enslaved Egyptians. Designed by Tartu-born Jacques Rosenbaum in 1910, it is by far Tallinn's most memorable Art Nouveau facade.

Brotherhood of Black Heads doorway

The bright, triple-gabled **Kanut Guild Hall** (Kanuti gildi hoone) stands next door at Pikk 20. This was home to the Kanut Guild, which united skilled craftspeople from a number of different trades. The house's current Tudor-style appearance comes from an 1860s remodelling, its overall look inspired by English Gothic architecture. The two bold-looking statues on its facade represent St Kanut and Martin Luther. The house is now used as a dance theatre (www.saal.ee).

High up, across the street from the Kanut Guild Hall, is the somewhat bizarre figure of a monocle-wearing man gazing down. There are several theories as to the sculpture's origins; the most amusing is that a jealous wife installed it to break her husband's habit of spying on the ladies as they practised ballet in the upper floors of the guild hall.

At Pikk 26 you come to the eye-catching **House of the Brotherhood of Black Heads** ⓴ (Mustpeade Maja; www.filharmoonia.ee/mustpeademaja; guided tours available). The brotherhood, a guild of young, unmarried merchants, played a major role in medieval Tallinn's life and politics, organising the town's defence and, among other duties, arranging annual tournaments and celebrations. The guild's curious name comes from the fact that its patron saint, St Mauritius, was a Moor. The exquisite Renaissance facade dates from 1597, and its beautiful carved-wood door – one of the most recognisable architectural elements in Tallinn – was installed in 1640. The house is now used as a concert hall, but in summer, when no events are scheduled, visitors can drop in to look at its gorgeous vaulted White Hall and Olav's Hall, as well as an intriguing indoor courtyard.

The Three Sisters

SOVIET INSIGHTS

Signs of the nation's Soviet past, some subtle, others blatant, are everywhere in Tallinn, but visitors with a particular interest in this chapter of the nation's history should keep a couple of opportunities in mind. The Vabamu Museum of Occupations and Freedom (www.vabamu.ee; charge) provides a high-tech and dramatic introduction to the 1940–91 period. The more humorous aspects of Soviet life come out at the *Viru Hotel* and its KGB Museum (www.viru.ee; €14). The hotel was the official stopping place for foreign guests to the city and as such was rife with intrigue. Its upper floor also housed a secret radio room. The museum can only be visited on a prebooked tour, but it's well worth the trouble for the hilarious stories and insights into everyday Soviet life it dishes out.

Further down the street, a careful observer will notice something eerie about the building at Pikk 59. Its cellar windows are completely bricked over – a detail that gives it a decidedly ominous appearance. This was the **KGB Headquarters** during the Soviet period. In this sad place many people were tortured and shot; others were interrogated before being sent to Siberia. A placard once mounted on the building read, 'Here stands the headquarters of the organ of repression of the Soviet Occupation – the road of suffering for Estonians.' After being inaccessible for years, the prison cells are now open (www.vabamu.ee; charge).

ST OLAV'S CHURCH

Just a few paces further on is Tallinn's largest medieval structure, the enormous **St Olav's Church** ⑮ (Oleviste kirik; www.oleviste.ee; free). A short walk around its side, towards Lai Street, will provide a better view of its sheer magnitude. The church was first mentioned in historic records in 1267 and originally served as a Scandinavian merchants' camp that occupied this end of Pikk Street in the

WHERE TO SHOOT THE BEST PICTURES

To capture that iconic cluster of red rooftops pierced by onion domes, climb the steep medieval steps up the church tower at St Olav's or St Mary's, though you could equally take the glass lift to the tip of the spire at the Niguliste Museum (see page 63). Walking the ancient ramparts provides its own money shot – specifically from Fat Margaret's Tower (see page 59), where you can snap Old Town in one direction and the port the other. All these require an entry fee, mind you. For a free crack at a million-euro Old Town view, visit the Kohtuotsa or Piiskopi viewing platforms on Toompea Hill. At 175 metres, the Tallinn TV Tower's observation deck puts those heights to shame (see page 77). Though the 360-degree views are less intimate here in Pirita, they do afford glimpses of Helsinki on clear days. In the opposite direction, Stroomi beach is as undeveloped as a far-flung Baltic island, yet barely fifty minutes from town by foot (ten by bus). The Mustjõe birdwatching tower is half a mile down the promenade, for unspoiled panoramas best captured at sunset.

thirteenth century. The basic shape it has today, however, comes from a rebuilding undertaken in the fifteenth century.

In 1500, an absurdly tall (159m/522ft) Gothic-style pavilion steeple was built onto the top of the tower, making St Olav's the tallest building in the world in 1549, when the spire of England's Lincoln Cathedral collapsed. The hope was that the huge steeple would act as a helpful signpost for ships approaching the busy commercial town. The steeple indeed proved to be a useful advertising tool, but it turned out to be even better as a lightning rod. Numerous bolts struck the spire through the centuries, and twice – once in 1625 and again in 1820 – the church was burned to the ground. The steeple you now see was installed after the first fire, and is only 124m (407ft) tall. Energetic visitors can make the arduous climb to the top of the **church tower** (charge) for spectacular views of Toompea and the Old Town.

THE GREAT COAST GATE AND VICINITY

Humbler in size than the church but just as awe-inspiring are the **Three Sisters** ⓰ (Kolm õde), at Pikk 71, a magnificently restored trio of brightly painted fifteenth-century terraced houses attached in a sibling-like way. The houses and their beautiful facades – including an intricate Baroque front door dating to 1651 – are striking examples of medieval architecture. The street ends at the **Great Coast Gate** ⓱ (Suur Rannavärav). This and the Viru Gates on Viru Street are all that remain of the six powerful medieval entryways that once regulated access to Tallinn. The Great Coast Gate – actually a collection of towers and gates – was founded in the early 1300s, but its largest and most famous piece, **Fat Margaret's Tower** (Paks Margareeta), was built between 1511 and 1530. The squat, round cannon tower is best viewed from outside the gate. With a diameter of 25m (82ft) and walls that were up to 5m (17ft) thick, the tower was a formidable part of the town's defences.

The tower now houses the **Estonian Maritime Museum** (Eesti Meremuuseum; www.meremuuseum.ee; charge); another branch of the museum is at the Seaplane Harbour (see page 69), with four floors of displays presenting the nation's seafaring history from Neolithic times to the present, and views of the

Fat Margaret's Tower

town and harbour from the roof. On the grassy hill outside the tower you'll see a row of medieval cannons, and a large monument in the shape of an incomplete bridge. The latter is a memorial to the victims of the *Estonia* ferry disaster. The 15,000-tonne ferry sank en route from Tallinn to Stockholm on 28 September 1994, resulting in 852 fatalities. From here, wooden steps lead down to Uus Street, from where you can reach Vene Street and the Latin Quarter.

THE LATIN QUARTER

The area at the end of Vene Street has come to be called Tallinn's Latin Quarter thanks to the presence of a Dominican Monastery that operated here between the thirteenth and sixteenth centuries. The monastery itself, or what remains of it, still defines the area, but these days a clutch of newer sights add to the fascinating milieu of this corner of the Old Town. One example can be found at the end of Vene Street in the form of the impressive **St Nicholas's Orthodox Church** (Püha Nikolai Imetegija kirik). This Neoclassical Russian Orthodox church, with its copper dome and double towers, was built in the 1820s by St Petersburg-based Swiss architect Luigi Rusca. Visitors shouldn't be afraid to look inside at the iconostasis, said to rival the most beautiful in Estonia. Across the street from the church, at Vene 17, a well-restored medieval house is home to the **Tallinn City Museum** (Tallinna Linnamuuseum; www.linnamuuseum.ee; charge). Well worth a visit, this extensive, modern museum chronicles the city's development from its founding right up to post-Soviet times. Vene Street's main feature is the **Dominican Monastery** ⓲ (Dominiklaste Klooster). Known as St Catherine's Monastery, it was founded

> **NOTES**
>
> During Soviet times, the neighbouring KGB office used St Olav's metal spire as an antenna for its radio communications.

St Catherine's Passage

here in 1246 by the Dominican Order, and until the Reformation, played a key role in the town's religious affairs. The monastery wasn't always popular with Tallinn's ruling elite, however, because the monks' work was often too supportive of the common Estonian people. The monastery was closed down after the Reformation in 1525, and in 1531 the abandoned complex was ravaged by fire.

Now all that remains of the monastery are the **courtyard** and a few of its surrounding hallways and chambers. In summer you can stroll along St Catherine's Passage (see below) to Müürivahe 33, site of the **Dominican Monastery Claustrum** (www.mauritanum. eu; charge). This institution gives access to the monastery's inner chambers, such as the prior's living quarters, monks' dormitory, library and refectory. The mysterious '**energy pillar**' in the cellar is believed to exude a kind of psychic force. Tallinn's most picturesque lane, **St Catherine's Passage** (Katariina käik), connects Vene and Müürivahe streets just south of the monastery. A long row of fifteenth- to seventeenth-century structures on one side of the passage houses **St Catherine's Guild** (Katariina gild; www.katariinagild.eu), where a group of female artists use traditional methods to create modern-looking and sometimes offbeat handicrafts. Visitors can drop in and watch the artisans working on quilts, ceramics, glass, silk designs, jewellery and fine leatherwork. The opposite side of the alleyway displays intriguing – if eerie – stone burial slabs that were removed from the St Catherine's Church directly behind them.

ST NICHOLAS CHURCH

St Nicholas Church ⓭ (Niguliste kirik), which looks proudly over Harju Street, was the only church in Lower Town not to be ransacked during the Reformation of 1524, thanks to its head of congregation, who successfully kept the mobs at bay by pouring molten lead into the locks. Dedicated to the patron saint of merchants and artisans, it was founded by a group of German settlers who had set up a trading yard here in the early thirteenth century. Because it was built before Tallinn's town wall was completed, the church was outfitted with heavy wooden beams to bar the doors and hiding places for those escaping attack. The main body and choir were modernised in the fifteenth century, though the church's current appearance is the result of constant rebuilding since then. The church was destroyed in the Soviet bombing raid of March 1944 and painstakingly reconstructed between 1956 and 1984.

St Nicholas's now serves a purely secular function, operating as the **Niguliste Museum and Concert Hall** (https://nigulistemuuseum.ekm.ee/en; charge), which showcases religious art from Estonia and abroad. Art lovers should definitely not pass up an opportunity to visit this fascinating church-turned-museum. It has the distinction of containing Estonia's most famous work of art, fifteenth-century artist Bernt Notke's mural **Dance Macabre** (*Dance with Death*), a frightening masterpiece depicting people from various walks of life dancing with skeletons. Other treasures

Dance of Death by Bernt Notke in St Nicholas's Orthodox Church

WORLD WAR II DESTRUCTION

Sharp-eyed travellers will notice that the side of Harju Street near St Nicholas Church is strangely devoid of buildings. This absence is a sad testament to the night of 9 March 1944, when approximately three hundred Soviet Army planes bombed Tallinn, killing more than 550 civilians, destroying entire neighbourhoods and leaving twenty percent of the population homeless. Locals often point out that, of the 3068 bombs dropped, not a single one hit a military target. The area of the Old Town hardest hit was Harju Street, where this entire block was reduced to rubble and remained mostly turfed over for the ensuing decades.

In 2007, as the city was redeveloping the area into a park and ice rink, it created a memorial to the bombing by unearthing and restoring Trepi tänav (Stairway Street), a lane that once ran between two buildings between Harju and the church. At its top is Needle-Eye Gate, partly reconstructed from its original pieces, which had been stored away in museums. Glass openings at the base of the street provide a glimpse into the cellars of the houses that once stood here.

in the museum include awe-inspiring altars from the sixteenth and seventeenth centuries, a collection of Renaissance and Baroque chandeliers and several curious tombstones from the fourteenth to seventeenth centuries. The museum also houses a **Silver Chamber** displaying exquisite ceremonial items from Tallinn's guilds. Making use of its wonderful acoustics, the church hosts **organ concerts** on weekend afternoons. A concert schedule is posted outside.

FREEDOM SQUARE

Freedom Square ⓴ (Vabaduse väljak), at the southern tip of the Old Town, is central Tallinn's 'other' main square. In striking contrast to its rival, Town Hall Square, it has a decidedly modern look. It was rescued from its decades-long status as a parking lot in 2009 when it underwent an extensive makeover and was returned to the townspeople. One of the additions during the makeover was the towering **War of Independence Victory Column** that dominates the square's western edge. Topped by a likeness of the Cross of Liberty medal, the glass-plated column is the centrepiece of a memorial to the country's 1918–20 struggle against Germany and Soviet Russia.

A look around the square will reveal multiple layers of the city's history. A glass viewing area at the Harju Street corner lets passers-by peer down at the underground remnants of the medieval Harju Gate. The late-nineteenth-century **St John's Church** (Jaani kirik) presides over the square's east side. Most other buildings visible here, including the hotel, Russian Drama Theatre and city offices across Karli Boulevard, reflect a definite 1930s style – a result of the prewar economic boom.

SCENIC PARKS

Linda Hill monument

Mysteriously overlooked by most visitors, the scenic parks and paths that ring the east side of the Old Town offer picture-perfect views of the town fortifications – not to mention a relaxing escape from the tourist crowds. The large green space that starts at Freedom Square and stretches nearly to Fat Margaret's Tower was once part of a system of bastions and moats that protected the town from attack. Now it's a favourite place for Tallinners of all ages to stroll.

Stenbock House aboce Schnelli Pond in Toompark

Starting from Freedom Square you can ascend the stone steps next to the victory column and then climb the paths to the peak of **Harju Hill** (Harjumägi) for views of the city. Working your way westward, past the Kiek in de Kök tower, you soon reach Toompea Street, from where you can either descend to the lower **Hirve Park** or continue along Falgi Street to the next rise, **Linda Hill** (Lindamägi). At its summit stands a solemn **monument** ㉑ to the mythical figure Linda, whose husband Kalev, according to ancient lore, founded the town (see page 37). The statue predates World War II, but what's significant about it is that Tallinn residents adopted it during Soviet times as a kind of unsanctioned memorial to loved ones deported to Siberia. Since there would be no gravesite and no official memorial, relatives would lay flowers here, at considerable risk to themselves if they were caught. Even now the tradition continues, and a plaque that has been added reads, 'To remember the ones who were taken away'.

From Linda Hill, cross Falgi and take the stairs downwards. From here, the view becomes more scenic with Toompea Castle and the sharp cliffs below joining the panorama. A jog to the left around the football pitch brings you to **Toompark** ㉒, whose paths and bridges surround **Schnelli Pond** (Schnelli tiik), the only remaining part of the town's water-filled moat. Finally, a walk through the **Square of Towers** ㉓ (Tornide väljak), another green pocket just north of Nunne Street, offers the best possible view of Tallinn's medieval wall and towers. In spring and summer, this is the site of the city's International Flower Festival, where you can tour elaborate and often outlandish natural arrangements. From here, a break in the wall opens the way back into Lower Town.

Patarei Prison

KALAMAJA

With its colourful wooden houses, offbeat galleries and popular cafés, the up-and-coming Kalamaja neighbourhood, just outside Old Town, presents the edgier side of the city's character, as well as some must-see sights. The part-residential, part-industrial area grew up in the late nineteenth and early twentieth centuries, when the coming of the railway sparked an influx of factories and workers. Thanks to this phenomenon, a quaint and curious hotchpotch of homes, in varying states of repair, now lines most of Kalamaja's quiet streets.

Start at the railway station, taking in the architecture along Vabriku, Valgevase and Töötuse streets, before making your way along Vana-Kalamaja towards the bay. The street ends at a staircase leading towards the ominous **Patarei Prison** ㉔ (Patarei Vangla). Originally built as a sea fortress in the early nineteenth century, it served as a prison and execution site through the Soviet era and was finally closed in 2002. Most of the sprawling territory has been left as it was, though some buildings now house art galleries and a summer-only seaside café. The **Prison Museum** (Vanglamuuseum; www.patareiprison.org), its hallways once dark and dank, is currently closed but set to reopen in 2026. To the west of the prison is

Torpedo tube, Lembit submarine

PROTO (Peetri 10; www.prototehas.ee; charge), a gigantic science museum displaying industrial-age inventions; don a VR headset and fly in a hot-air balloon, or play an organ to power an electric transformer invented by Nikola Tesla.

Nearby is Kalamaja's biggest attraction, the **Seaplane Harbour** ㉕ (Lennusadam; www.meremuuseum.ee/lennusadam; charge), a branch of the Estonian Maritime Museum (see page 59). This museum and activity centre makes its home in and around a set of domed seaplane hangars dating to World War I. The vast interior displays boats, mines and anti-aircraft guns, while hands-on exhibitions let visitors attempt to shoot down helicopters, make paper airplanes and try on old military uniforms. Pride of place in the hall is given to the *Lembit* **submarine**, built in Barrow-in-Furness, England, in 1936 for the Estonian Navy and later co-opted into the Soviet fleet. Visitors can climb inside to inspect the torpedo hatches and crew members' bunks.

The outdoor exhibit comprises a handful of ships that can be toured, including the *Suur Tõll* **icebreaker**, built in 1914, the largest intact steam-powered icebreaker in the world.

Just beyond the Seaplane Harbour is a further attention-grabbing example of suburban Tallinn's efforts at postindustrial reinvention, the **Noblessner Quarter** (https://noblessner.ee), occupying the former shipyard of Emanuel Nobel and Arthur Lessner. With factory halls transformed into offices, apartments, shops and restaurants, all broken up by pedestrian-friendly piazzas, it's another striking showcase of contemporary Estonia at work and play. Here you will find the **Punctum Gallery** (Allveelaeva 4; https://punctum.ee; free), whose exhibitions focus on photography and contemporary art by Baltic creatives.

From the harbour and prison area, a paved pathway called the 'Cultural Kilometer' follows the shoreline east towards the Passenger Harbour, ending at the Culture Cauldron, an art centre housed in a former heating plant. The **Estonian Museum of**

Contemporary Art (EKKM; www.ekkm.ee; free) that makes its home here shows off the generation's latest creations. Students of architecture might also want to climb the nearby **Linnahall** ㉖ (www.linnahall.ee; free), a hulking, concrete monstrosity built in 1980 as a port and events centre. The structure is a stellar example of Soviet design and excess.

KADRIORG

HIGHLIGHTS

» Kadriorg Palace, see page 71
» Kumu, see page 72
» Kadriorg Park, see page 73

The Rotermann Quarter

ROTERMANN QUARTER

By far the best place to see how Tallinn is putting a contemporary spin on its industrial heritage and breathing new life into once-rundown buildings is the Rotermann Quarter (Rotermanni Kvartal), located between Old Town and the Passenger Port. The former factory area has been thoroughly revamped into a shopping and culture zone complete with restaurants, galleries and a busy event area. The inventive architecture alone makes it worth a visit. While here, drop into the Rotermanni Salt Storage building at Ahtri 2. This distinctive example of a limestone building from 1908 houses the Museum of Estonian Architecture (www.arhitektuurimuuseum.ee; charge), with rotating exhibitions on the most iconic architecture of the nation's past eras.

For Tallinn natives, the name Kadriorg evokes images of nature, art and imperial Russian extravagance. This leafy neighbourhood of parks, ponds and villas just outside the city centre owes its existence to Tsar Peter the Great, who established a summer estate here in the early eighteenth century soon after conquering Estonia in the Great Northern War. He named the estate in honour of his wife, Catherine I – 'Kadriorg' means 'Catherine's Valley' in Estonian.

In the nineteenth century, wealthy Tallinn residents began to build grand, wooden villas in the area, and in the 1920s and 1930s, chic, functionalist houses started to appear. Through the years, the area kept its upper-class appeal and it remains one of Tallinn's most prestigious neighbourhoods, as well as a favourite place to spend a relaxing afternoon – all the more so because it is now home to several of the nation's top art museums.

KADRIORG PALACE

The jewel in the Kadriorg's crown is the lavish, Baroque **Kadriorg Palace** ㉗ (Kadrioru loss), built on the order of Peter the Great in 1718. Designed by Niccolo Michetti, an Italian architect who also worked on the famous Peterhof near St Petersburg, the palace is laid out in Italian villa style: a main building flanked by two annexes. The Tsar named it Ekaterinenthal, or Catherinenthal, in honour of his wife, and intended to use it as a summer residence, though in the end his family spent hardly any time here.

Its two-storey **main hall**, decorated with rich stuccowork and grandiose ceiling paintings, is considered one of the finest examples of Baroque design in Northern Europe. Behind the building, the carefully manicured eighteenth-century-style **flower garden**, with its shooting fountains, is equally impressive.

As the building is itself a masterpiece, it is appropriate that it houses the **Kadriorg Art Museum** (https://kadriorumuuseum.ekm.ee; charge), which exhibits the Estonian Art Museum's foreign art collection. Here, precious paintings by Western European and Russian artists of the sixteenth to twentieth centuries are on display, as are prints, sculptures and superb works in metal and porcelain.

While in the area, those interested in art should also visit the **Mikkel Museum** (https://mikkelimuuseum.ekm.ee; charge), just across the street in what used to be the palace's kitchen building. Donated by private collector Johannes Mikkel in 1994, the exquisite works include Flemish and Dutch paintings, Italian engravings and Chinese porcelain. The pride and joy of the collection is a set of four etchings by Rembrandt, one of which is a self-portrait.

Up the hill, just above the palace garden, is the Presidential Palace, the office and residence of Estonia's head of state. Built in 1938, this palace is relatively modest compared to the neighbouring Kadriorg Palace, which had previously fulfilled this role. Though tourists aren't allowed inside, they may take photos of the exterior and of the honour guards standing at the front.

KUMU

At the top end of Weizenbergi stands the poster child of all the city's art museums, the **Kumu** ㉘ (https://kumu.ekm.ee; charge). The vast

Kadriorg Palace

ahead-of-the-curve art and cultural centre has a focus on Estonian art, displaying works by the nation's top creative talents through history. It also serves as the main building of the Art Museum of Estonia.

The unique building itself makes a visit here worthwhile. Designed by Finnish architect Pekka Vapaavuori and partially built into a limestone cliff, it looks like a work of science fiction brought to life, both inside and out.

KADRIORG PARK ATTRACTIONS

The sprawling **Kadriorg Park** ㉙ that surrounds Kadriorg Palace encompasses open spaces, wooded areas, statues, benches, paths and ponds. By far the most dazzling of the park's sights is the large, rectangular **Swan Pond** adjacent to Weizenbergi Street, near the palace. The symmetrical pond with fountains and

A ceiling fresco at Kadriorg Palace

a beautiful white gazebo at its centre could easily set the scene for a Tchaikovsky ballet. Here, swans, ducks and pigeons all vie for the breadcrumbs that local children invariably throw, while their parents wander nearby, admiring the colourful flowerbeds that line the surrounding paths.

One of these paths leads southeast towards the Kumu, passing a children's play park before reaching a stairway and fountain area that is just as beautiful as the Swan Pond.

Over the street and running in front of the palace, a long, straight path leads towards the seashore and to a magnificent statue of an angel standing on a large stone pedestal, gazing out to sea. This is the **Russalka Memorial**, built to commemorate the 177 men lost when the Russian warship *Russalka* sank en route from Tallinn to Helsinki in 1893. Russian-speaking couples traditionally lay flowers at the foot of this dramatic monument on their wedding day. From here, a 2km (3-mile) skate and bike path stretches along the rim of the bay, passing Maarjamäe and ending at Pirita Beach. Back over the wide road, slightly further down the coast, is the entrance to the **Song Festival Grounds** (Lauluväljak), home to Estonia's Song Festival, held every five years. It was here that the Singing Revolution began (see page 29), when hundreds of thousands of Estonians gathered to sing traditional songs as a mass demonstration against Soviet dominance. Built in 1960 and with a distinctive, curving roof, the **Song Festival Arena** is Tallinn's largest outdoor stage.

OUTLYING AREAS

HIGHLIGHTS

- » Maarjamäe, see page 75
- » Pirita, see page 76
- » Estonian Open Air Museum, see page 79

MAARJAMÄE

This coastal hill just north of Kadriorg is a fascinating spot for visitors interested in World War II and Soviet history.

First and foremost, this is the site of the sprawling **Maarjamäe War Memorial** ➌, an impossibly ugly and overbearing cement-filled park that could only have been born of the Soviet 1960s and 1970s. Its concrete avenues and abstract iron sculptures were installed in 1975 to commemorate Soviet soldiers killed in Estonia during World War II. Many a semi-mandatory, enthusiastic Soviet rally was held at the now-crumbling amphitheatre here. Ironically, the memorial is built on what had earlier been a German cemetery, now marked by the solemn crosses visible behind the complex.

Nearby stands the **Maarjamäe Palace** (Maarjamäe loss), a grand pseudo-Gothic manor built by Count Orlov-Davidov in

1874. Originally used as a summer home, the 'palace' changed hands several times through the years, serving as a Dutch consul's residence, a prestigious hotel, an aviation school and even a Soviet army barracks. The building now houses the branch of the **Estonian History Museum** (www.ajaloomuuseum.ee; charge) that focuses on the birth of the Estonian Republic, the occupation years and the second independence. It is also home to the **Estonian Film Museum**.

PIRITA

Pirita, a ten-minute drive north of the centre, is Tallinn's favourite summer playground, mainly thanks to the immensely popular **Pirita Beach** ㉛, a vast stretch of sand invariably packed with tanning bodies and frolicking children on any warm day. The forested, mostly residential district also claims a number of other notable attractions, ranging from the captivatingly scenic to the grandly Soviet.

Squarely in the first category are the spectacular ruins of **St Bridget's Convent** ㉜ (Pirita klooster; www.piritaklooster.ee; free). Founded by the Swedish Bridgettine Order in 1407, the convent operated here until Ivan the Terrible's forces destroyed it in 1577. What remains are the convent's towering, gabled facade, the walls of its main building, several foundations, cellars and a cemetery.

Beyond the ruins, the tranquil **Pirita River** slowly winds its way through the district before emptying out into Tallinn Bay. Pedal boats, rowing boats and canoes can be rented by the hour from **Pirita Boat Rental** (Paadilaenutus; http://bellmarine.ee; charge), operating from the built-up embankment, downhill from the convent. A leisurely row or pedalo ride is a perfect way to experience the lush, marshy beauty of the area.

In the Kloostrimetsa section of Pirita, about 3km (2 miles) from the beach, is a plant-lover's paradise, the **Tallinn Botanical Gardens** ㉝ (Tallinna Botaanikaaed; www.botaanikaaed.ee; charge). More than eight thousand plant species can be found on

Pirita Beach

its 123 hectares (300 acres) of landscaped grounds and its greenhouses display everything from rare varieties to houseplants.

Joint tickets are available for the Botanical Gardens and this area's other main attraction, the space-age-looking **Tallinn TV Tower** ❸❹ (Teletorn; www.teletorn.ee; charge). The gargantuan structure dates to the Soviet 1980s but was given a thorough update decades later. At 314m (1030ft), it is by far the tallest structure in town. You may have to queue at peak times before boarding the super-fast lift to the observation deck at the 175m (575ft) level, but it is worth the wait. Unforgettable 360-degree views of the city and surrounding ports unfold from here, and those who don't suffer from vertigo are even encouraged to stand on patches of glass flooring. The tower also features a brasserie-style café-restaurant, a 3D film, an exhibition about the tower's history and another about world-famous Estonians.

Estonian Open Air Museum

BALTI JAAM AND TELLISKIVI

North of the Old Town, the busy **Balti Jaam market** (Balti Jaama turg; https://en.astri.ee) provides the city with most of its fresh fruit and veg, and also offers flowers, chocolates, delicatessen products and handicrafts. A short walk further north, a former factory site has been reimagined as the cool **Telliskivi Creative City** (https://telliskivi.cc/en), where a cluster of creative businesses, design stores, cafés and boutique shops is grouped around a courtyard. It is home to **Fotografiska Tallinn** (Telliskivi tn 60a-8; www.tallinn.fotografiska.com; charge), whose ahead-of-the-curve photography exhibitions shine a light on emerging and established talent like Alison Jackson and Yang Fudong. The museum's rooftop restaurant is just as forward-thinking, with its zero-waste approach, and has been awarded a Michelin Green star for its efforts.

ESTONIAN OPEN AIR MUSEUM

Rocca al Mare, once a private seaside estate on the western edge of Kopli Bay, is now home to one of Tallinn's most unique tourist attractions, the **Estonian Open Air Museum** ㉟ (Eesti Vabaõhumuuseum; www.evm.ee; charge). Dozens of thatch-roofed farmhouses, barns, windmills and watermills dating back to the eighteenth century combine to give a vivid impression of what Estonian village life must have been like in times past. Characters dressed in period costume drive horse carts through the park, others perform chores while visitors look on. One of the mandatory stops here is the *Kolu Tavern*, famous for its traditional Estonian pea soup.

Visitors should set aside at least half a day to tour the park properly. Those with children in tow should also note that the **Tallinn Zoo** (see page 105) is in the same part of town.

EXCURSIONS

HIGHLIGHTS
- » Lahemaa National Park, see page 80
- » Jägala Waterfall, see page 83
- » Naissaar, Aegna and Prangli, see page 83
- » Pärnu, see page 84
- » Tartu, see page 87
- » Haapsalu, see page 90

A day-trip from Tallinn will allow you to experience the rugged splendour of Estonia's countryside or explore one of the nation's other notable cities, each of which has a history and spirit quite different from those of the capital. For visitors with more time on their hands, hiring a car is a good way to see the country. That said, it is not essential. Convenient buses connect Tallinn to the cities mentioned below, and organised tours are available for out-of-the-way locations.

A pretty forest near Käsmu

LAHEMAA NATIONAL PARK

Along the northern coast, about an hour's drive east of Tallinn, unfurls Estonia's largest nature reserve, **Lahemaa National Park** (Lahemaa rahruspark), a perfect antidote to urban tourism. The 725 sq km (280 sq mile) park encompasses vast sweeps of forest, jagged seashores, wetlands and several historic villages, as well as some stunning seventeenth- and eighteenth-century manor houses.

Your first stop should be **Palmse Manor** (Palmse Mõis), the most striking manor house in the country. Completed in 1740, it was home to the von der Pahlen family until 1919, when a land-reform law nationalised the manorial holdings and divided them among local farmers. The house then served as a convalescent home and later a Soviet pioneer camp, but it has since been renovated and now operates as a museum (www.virumaamuuseumid.ee/en/

palmse-manor; charge). Visitors are welcome to stroll through the manor grounds, where they'll find a peaceful swan pond and landscaped gardens.

The manor also serves as Lahemaa's **Visitor Centre** (http://loodusegakoos.ee). In the stable-carriage house you'll find maps and information on the park's sights and nature walks.

Not far away is another impressive manor house, **Sagadi Manor**, now a hotel. It was built in 1749, but renovated at the end of that century in a Neoclassical style. As with Palmse, the complex is open to visitors and its interior contains a museum. One of its outbuildings also houses a forestry museum (http://sagadi.ee/museum; charge).

Lahemaa's other attractions include a string of hamlets, including **Altja**, a lovely Estonian fishing village. The old wooden buildings were restored in the 1970s, and the village has since become a popular local tourist spot. Here you'll find a nineteenth-century inn, a traditional village swing and walking paths along the coast.

Another coastal village, **Käsmu**, is less typical. This one has a decidedly affluent look as a result of its residents' salt-smuggling activities in the nineteenth century. In the 1920s, when Finland imposed prohibition, the economic focus here naturally shifted to alcohol. Apart from the houses of wealthy sea captains, Käsmu

The swan pond at Palmse Manor

The spectacular Jägala Waterfall

is known for its **Maritime Museum** (www.kasmu.ee; free), housed in what was once a school of navigation.

Like Käsmu, the village of **Viinistu** also profited from alcohol smuggling, but what puts it on the map nowadays is something else entirely. This village of just 150 people is home to the **Viinistu Art Museum** (www.viinistu.ee/en/museum; charge), which has the largest private art collection in Estonia. The nineteenth- and twentieth-century Estonian paintings on display easily rival those of the state-owned museums in Tallinn. This anomaly is thanks to one former resident who, as a child, fled with his family to Sweden during World War II. After making his fortune as manager of the pop group ABBA, he returned to Viinistu, eventually converting a Soviet-era fish collective into this art centre. Apart from the museum, the village has a respectable tavern and a small trail that follows the coastline.

JÄGALA WATERFALL

On the way to Lahemaa, visitors can take a small detour north from the Narva Highway to the village of Jägala-Joa, home to one of Estonia's best-known beauty spots, the **Jägala Waterfall** ❸. About 8m (26ft) high and at times up to 70m (230ft) wide, the waterfall is given its uniquely spectacular look by the way the river pours over the edge of a perfectly flat limestone shelf. The exposed cliff face reveals more layers of limestone, a geological feature for which northern Estonia is famous. Through the centuries, the waterfall has cut a gorge that is 300m (980ft) long and 12 to 14m (39 to 46ft) deep.

NAISSAAR, AEGNA AND PRANGLI

Strictly summer destinations, these three forested islands off the Tallinn coast offer opportunities to experience the serenity of Estonian nature as well as glimpse some truly curious aspects of the nation's past. Visiting each requires planning and is best done with the help of a tour operator. The most easily accessible is **Naissaar**, or Women's Island, about 10km (6 miles) from the mainland. Sunlines (www.sunlines.ee) and Monica Ferries (www.monica.ee) operate ferry connections, tours and excursions.

Since the late 1990s most of the island has been a nature reserve, but for nearly fifty years it was a closed Soviet naval base whose main function was the manufacture of sea mines. Military sites around the island include the abandoned mine factory, a ghost town that once housed Soviet military personnel, and the remains of concrete bunkers. Trails also take visitors to the island's two **lighthouses**, and past **cemeteries** where English and French soldiers from the Crimean War are buried.

The island is 11km (7 miles) long and 4km (2.5 miles) wide and can be explored on foot or by bicycle (rental at the dock). The **Nature Park Centre**, uphill from the dock, provides maps to the two main **trails**. The island's only village, **Männiku**, is about twenty minutes on foot from the port and has a restaurant and

Pärnu, Tallinn's summer capital

guesthouse. From here, a narrow-gauge railway operates for tourists.

Aegna, Tallinn's 'picnic island', is a quarter of the size of Naissaar and was also militarised during the Soviet period. Its main attraction is now its tranquillity, with hiking trails, beaches, an old cemetery and a 'magical stone maze' among its prominent features. Sunlines (www.sunlines.ee) makes the one-hour crossing from Tallinn's Kalasadam (summer only).

Unlike the other two islands, **Prangli** was spared from wartime depopulation. Thanks to this, it has been able to preserve a traditional fishing culture with roots going back six centuries. In addition to seeing what village life is like for the island's 150 residents, visitors are treated to pristine beaches, pine forests and a museum. Prangli Travel (www.pranglireisid.ee) runs full-service excursions (summer only).

PÄRNU

Each year when the seasons change and the weather finally starts warm up, Estonians like to abandon their dreary offices and schoolrooms and head off to **Pärnu** ㊲, their 'summer capital' on a coastal inlet 129km (80 miles) south of Tallinn. This quiet resort town of 40,000 inhabitants is known for its leafy parks, health spas, quaint town centre and, most of all, its long stretch of white sandy beach.

Though Pärnu is over 750 years old and has witnessed numerous changes of empire, its most relevant history starts in 1838, when the town's first health spa was established. Thanks to the therapeutic properties of the town's mud treatments, pleasant weather and sea air, Pärnu quickly grew into a popular spa destination – a tradition that continues today. Now it can claim six spa hotels offering everything from plastic surgery to water slides.

When most travellers first arrive in Pärnu, they find themselves in the historic downtown area, the centrepiece of which is **Rüütli Street**. This long, pedestrian walkway and the few streets that surround it are home to numerous cafés, boutiques and a hotchpotch of intriguing buildings dating from the seventeenth to twentieth centuries. The most impressive of these landmarks are the imposing **Eliisabeti Church** from 1747, the dazzling Orthodox **Ekateriina Church** from 1768, and the mid-seventeenth-century **Almshouse** (Seegi maja), which now operates as a hotel and restaurant. Another notable seventeenth-century structure, the **Tallinn Gate** (Tallinna väravad), marks what used to be the road to Tallinn before the Pärnu River was finally spanned in 1938. Pärnu's oldest building is the **Red Tower** (Punane torn), a squat fifteenth-century edifice that once guarded the edge of town. Now painted white, it is hidden in an alley adjacent to Hommiku Street.

A couple of blocks north of the historic area, at Aida 3, the **Pärnu Museum** (www.parnu-muuseum.ee; charge) offers a comprehensive history of the town's development. Ringing downtown on the south and

> **NOTES**
>
> Because the Baltic Sea is virtually enclosed by land, it is environmentally extremely sensitive. It takes around 35 years for all the water in the sea to be replaced by water from the ocean beyond. If any pollutants enter the water, they will stay there for two to three decades, by which time they may have severely damaged the area's ecosystems.

The pink Town Hall in Tartu

east is a well-developed park and marina area. Its flowerbeds, fountains and paths make it an excellent place to relax or stroll. On the streets nearby you can find a smattering of old, wooden villas and functionalist houses from the prewar period.

A few minutes' walk south brings you to Pärnu's true centre of gravity: the **beach**. Cafés, volleyball nets, ice-cream vendors, lifeguards and all the other trappings of a typical world-class beach can be found here. The only things lacking are crashing waves and sharks. When you tire of bronzing yourself on the sand, take time to see the area's treasures. The **Beach House** (Rannahoone), with a distinctive mushroom-shaped balcony, dates from 1939 and is a wonderful example of functionalism. The same can be said of the striking **Beach Hotel** (Rannahotell; www.rannahotell.ee) nearby, completed in 1937. The Neoclassical **Pärnu Mud Bath** (Pärnu Mudaravila), a symbol of the town with a dome-shaped roof and circular garden, is now a spa hotel (www.hedonspa.com), as is the luxury **Ammende Villa** (http://ammende.ee), housed in an Art Nouveau mansion slightly further away down Mere Puiestee. Also adjacent to the beach is the **Beach Park** (Rannapark), established in 1882. Slowly meander through the park and contemplate the scenery, or hire a pair of roller skates at the beach and rocket along its many paved paths.

TARTU

Its nickname is 'the city of good thoughts'. However, a better name for **Tartu** ⓷, a minor metropolis 189km (118 miles) southeast of Tallinn, might be 'the city of good ideas'. Tartu is Estonia's intellectual capital, home not only to the nation's largest and most prestigious educational institution, Tartu University, but also to several colleges, research centres and the nation's supreme court.

The atmosphere here is decidedly different from that in Tallinn: less rushed, more contemplative and, thanks to its student population, visibly younger. With 97,000 inhabitants, this is Estonia's second-largest city, but Tartu is still small enough to lack the annoyances found in many urban areas. At the same time, it has a clutch of cafés, parks, museums and historic sites – and just as interesting as any you could find in the capital.

Kissing Students fountain in Town Hall Square

As in Tallinn, the heart of Tartu is its **Old Town**, where the city's most striking architecture is concentrated. Unlike Tallinn, though, Tartu's Old Town no longer has a medieval look. Constant wars during the seventeenth century and the Great Fire of 1775 mean that most of what you see here was built in the late eighteenth and nineteenth centuries. Your first stop should be **Town Hall Square** (Raekoja plats), the centre of Tartu from time immemorial. The **Town Hall**

(Raekoda) presiding over the top of the square was opened in 1786 and its design reflects a mixture of early classicism, Baroque and rococo. The building is home to the **Visitor Centre** (www.visittartu.com). The whimsical fountain directly in front of the Town Hall, *Kissing Students*, is a relatively recent installation but has already become a favourite symbol of the town.

Further down the square is Tartu's Leaning Tower of Pisa, the **Tartu Art Museum** (www.tartmus.ee; charge), which tilts bizarrely to the left due to the soft riverbank mud on which it stands. The nearby **arched bridge** over the Emajõgi River replaced the eighteenth-century stone bridge that was destroyed in 1944. Taking a daring walk over the bridge's top rail has become a tradition among local students.

Just off the square from the Town Hall you'll find one of the most outstanding examples of Neoclassical architecture in Estonia, the **Tartu University Main Building**. Swedish King Gustav Adolph established Tartu University in 1632, and this structure was completed in 1809. The building houses an art museum (charge) whose collection of antiquities includes a 4000-year-old Egyptian mummy, plus an impressive concert hall and a Student Lock-up, where pupils were incarcerated for bad conduct. Not far away is Old Town's principal church, **St John's Church** (Jaani Kirik), which dates back to the late twelfth century and is renowned for its thousand-plus terracotta figures.

A short climb up **Toome Hill** (Toomemägi) brings you to the towering brick ruins of **Dome Cathedral**. Built in the thirteenth century, the cathedral served as the centre of a regional bishopric prior to the Reformation. Fire destroyed it in 1624. A restored section now houses the extensive **Museum of Tartu University History** (www. muuseum.ut.ee; charge), which displays old lab equipment, photos and the like. Some of the cathedral towers are also open for exploration April to November. On another crest of the hill stands Tartu's **Old Observatory** (charge), which began operations in 1810 and housed the most advanced telescope of its time. It now shelters a museum displaying antique stargazing devices and an old-fashioned planetarium show. Visitors can turn the rotating dome roof and climb outside for city views. Afterwards, stop for a pint at the nearby **Vilde Ja Vine** (www.vilde.ee), a richly decorated haunt in a historic printing house. A statue in front of the pub depicts a fictional chance meeting of Oscar Wilde (1854–1900) and the Estonian writer Eduard Wilde (1865–1933) on a park bench. An identical monument, a gift from Estonia in 2004, can be found in central Galway. For travellers with children, no visit to Tartu would be complete without a trip to the high-tech **AHHAA Science Centre** (www.ahhaa.ee; charge), a vast complex filled with clever, hands-on experiments and activities.

AHHAA Science Centre, Tartu

The seaside resort town of Haapsalu

HAAPSALU

Haapsalu ⓳, a seaside town 101km (63 miles) southwest of Tallinn, provides an insight into small-town life in Estonia. Early-twentieth-century wooden houses dominate Haapsalu's central neighbourhoods, many of its narrow streets have never been paved, and its residents seem to amble about in a particularly unhurried manner. At the same time, this resort town, which competes with Pärnu for the title of having the nation's most therapeutic mud, is home to enough historic curiosities to make a trip here worthwhile for anyone with a day to spare.

Haapsalu's best-known attraction is the late thirteenth-century **Episcopal Castle** that looms above the town centre. The castle served as both religious outpost and military fortress until Peter the Great conquered it at the beginning of the eighteenth century.

Though it mostly lies in ruins, much of the structure is still intact and visitors are free to stroll through its grassy courtyard and examine its remaining walls and old cannons. In summer, one section operates as a **museum** (www.linnus.salm.ee; charge), chronicling the town's history.

> **NOTES**
>
> People from all over the world come looking for cures from Haapsalu's sea mud. News of its efficacy was spread by Carl Abraham Hunnius, a military doctor who founded the first mud treatment centre here in 1825. It wasn't long before the fashionable folk of St Petersburg were making their way to Haapsalu.

One part of the castle that's not in ruins is the **Haapsalu Cathedral** (www.haapsalu.eelk.ee; free), whose beautiful interior you can see if you tour the castle's museum. One of the church's windows is central to the town's favourite legend, The White Lady of Haapsalu. The ghostly figure of a woman, who was supposedly immured in the castle walls, is said to appear at the window on moonlit nights in August. An annual White Lady Days music festival is named after the legend.

Not far from here is the town's seaside **promenade**, a good place for a stroll. Here you'll see a grand-looking, wooden **Resort Hall** (Kuursaal), and a five-minute walk along the esplanade, a **stone bench** that, with the help of modern technology, talks and plays classical music. This is a monument to the composer Pyotr Tchaikovsky, who supposedly was struck by inspiration for *Swan Lake* while holidaying in Haapsalu.

Rail enthusiasts should head to the **Railway and Communications Museum** (www.salm.ee; charge). Built into Haapsalu's romantic, early-twentieth-century railway station, the small museum displays a replica stationmaster's room, passengers' waiting room and a number of tools and uniforms. Outside on the tracks is a collection of locomotives and engines from the 1940s and 1950s.

Antiques at a Tallinn flea market

Things to do

During the height of the tourist season, live, outdoor entertainment is not just easy to find in Tallinn, it's nearly impossible to escape. Every kind of music, from traditional Estonian folk to Scottish bagpipes, echoes through the air as small, seemingly impromptu concerts erupt on squares and street corners in the Old Town.

The most uniquely Estonian events are those involving national song and dance. Generally, these folk performances are held only when specific festivals are scheduled, but if you happen to see groups of women wearing brightly striped village skirts, follow them to their concert and you'll be rewarded with beautiful, rural music traditions that go back hundreds of years.

CULTURE

National concert organiser Eesti Kontsert acts as a kind of one-stop-shop for Tallinn's classical performances. The company sells tickets for a whole spectrum of classical entertainment from its box office in the **Estonia Concert Hall** (www.estonia.concert.ee). Opera (www.opera.ee/en) and ballet tickets are sold in another part of the same building. Larger classical events take place in the theatre itself or in the nearby **Alexela Concert Hall** (www.kontserdimaja.ee), while medieval churches, guildhalls and towers provide interesting venues for the smaller shows. **Modern dance performances** take place in the Kanuti Guildhall (www.saal.ee).

For a change from the usual *Swan Lake* and *La Traviata*, buy tickets to any show by Tallinn's early-music ensemble, **Hortus Musicus** (www.concert.ee/en/collectives/hortus-musicus), whose repertoire of Baroque and Renaissance music complements the city's historic ambience. **Organ concerts**, held on Saturday and Sunday afternoons in St Nicholas Church (www.nigulistemuuseum.ekm.ee/en/concerts), offer more casual classical performance options. Concert times are posted outside the church.

LIVE MUSIC

> **NOTES**
>
> In summer you will find a classical concert or dance performance in Tallinn just about every night of the week. For an up-to-date list of what's happening on the cultural front, check the city tourist office's homepage (www.visittallinn.ee).

The city's small but spirited live-music scene mainly revolves around its bars and clubs, but every so often stand-alone concerts take place, usually in connection with one of the city's music festivals. Major international stars usually visit Tallinn when their European tours bring them to this part of the continent. In all cases, advertisements posted around the city will make sure you know what's going on. To see what events are scheduled ahead of your trip, check the Piletilevi ticket agency's website (www.piletilevi.ee), which also gives information about buying tickets offers an online booking system.

CINEMA

Cinema is an easy entertainment option in Tallinn as films are nearly always shown in their original language, with Estonian subtitles. The eleven-screen Apollo Kino Coca-Cola Plaza (www.apollokino.ee) screens mainly Hollywood fare, as does the Apollo Kino Solaris. The Sõprus (www.kinosoprus.ee) and Artis (www.kino.ee) concentrate on art-house films. Check www.kinoafisha.info for all show times and information in English.

NIGHTLIFE

There is absolutely no better way to relax in Tallinn than to sit at an outdoor café, beer in hand, watching the world meander past. Fortunately, the city also has a wide spectrum of nightlife to explore – everything from quiet, sophisticated lounges to pulsing dance clubs.

Like everything else in Tallinn, most nightlife is squeezed into the Old Town streets, giving rise to popular bar-hopping custom.

Since the bars are literally only a few paces apart, locals often change locations after every round, exploring all the area's options until they finally choose a place to settle in.

The bar-packed area around Suur-Karja and Väike-Karja becomes party central at weekends, with crowds, hubbub and drinks spilling out onto the streets. **Nimeta Baar** (Suur-Karja 4; https://nimetabaar.ee) is at the centre of the action and is popular among the young tourist set. Beer aficionados should head to **Brewklyn** in Port Noblessner, which runs promotions throughout the year and often hauls out the barbecue to round out the experience, or the **Drink Baar & Grill** (Väike-Karja 8; www.facebook.com/DrinkBaarAndGrill), where over eighty carefully selected brews are available. More local flavour can be found at the ever-popular **Hell**

Women in traditional Estonian folk outfits

Hunt (Pikk 39; www.hellhunt.ee), which has a great atmosphere and its own brand of beer.

For trendy, lounge-type surroundings, **Butterfly Lounge** (Vana-Viru 13; http://kokteilibaar.ee) is a good choice, as is **Whisper Sister** (www.whispersister.ee), a speakyeasy hidden in a historic building on Pärnu mnt. Cosy wine bars have also become fashionable. Try **Veino** (Suurtüki 2; www.instagram.com/veinoveinikas), which focuses on natural wines, or **Pan y Vino** (Pikk 34; www.panyvino.ee), a rustic Peruvian wine bar that also does a killer pisco sour.

Many of the larger bars and pubs offer live music at weekends, but some venues are particularly sought out for late-night entertainment. **Uus Laine** (Vana-Kalamaja tn 1) has a local rock, pop or funk act on nearly every night of the week, plus a weekly music quiz. **Von Krahli** (Telliskivi tn 60a-9; www.vonkrahl.ee) is the place to go for alternative theatre, live music and local beers on tap. They're both located just outside Old Town, in the burgeoning Telliskivi Creative City near the central train station.

Nightclubs are also easy to find, but hard to recommend. Crowds are fickle, so what could be full of life on one night could be desolate the next. One that is always popular, however, is the huge techno club **Hall** (Peetri 6; www.facebook.com/HallTallinn), which draws a young crowd to trendy Kalamaja. **Fonoteek** (www.fonoteek.ee), part of the burgeoning Telliskivi Creative City near the station, is part dance hall, part open-air beer garden.

> **NOTES**
>
> Expat-run Comedy Estonia organises frequent English-language stand-up events in pubs and clubs where aspiring locals, as well as foreign guest acts, work the crowds. See www.comedyestonia.com for the schedule.

SHOPPING

The explosive growth in Tallinn's retail sector over the past decade means you will have absolutely no trouble stuffing your suitcase with

Tallinn's knitwear market, or 'sweater wall'

gifts, souvenirs and other goodies. More shops and boutiques blossom with each new tourist season, and several shopping malls crowd the downtown area. What's more, all but the smallest locations will happily accept your plastic.

Despite these huge improvements in the shopping culture, however, Estonia is still a fairly secluded market, which means that not everything here is a bargain. Clothes, for example, can actually cost more in Tallinn than in relatively rich Scandinavia. Likewise, electronics are rarely a good deal. The upshot is that you cannot assume anything is cheaper here, and comparing prices to what you'd pay at home is crucial if you want to avoid spending blunders.

Nevertheless, with some products, you can almost always find good value. Locally made handicrafts, art and Estonian-produced fashion are a safe bet. Additionally, alcohol and cigarettes are typically a steal here because Estonia does not tax these items nearly as much as neighbouring countries do. This explains why Finnish beer is so much cheaper in Estonia than in Finland, and why the ferry back to Helsinki is always crowded with bleary-eyed karaoke stars.

WHERE TO SHOP

Without a doubt, the Old Town holds the most promise for intrepid souvenir-hunters. This area has by far the highest concentration of shops specialising in linen, glass, ceramics, knitwear and other authentic, locally made wares. Similarly, establishments offering antiques, art and traditional handicrafts line just about every street, especially those nearest Town Hall Square. General *suveniir* stores will sell the classic T-shirts and postcards, and are often crammed with mass-produced Russian dolls and the like. In short, almost anywhere you are in the Old Town, you'll be able to find shopping within a few metres.

Christmas market in Tallinn

Outdoor markets, while not actually common in Tallinn, present the most interesting shopping experience. First and foremost is the much-loved **knitwear market** along the old city wall on Müürivahe Street, near the Viru Gates. Since it doesn't have an official name, most foreigners simply refer to it as the **Sweater Wall**. Here, local artisans sell just about every kind of knitted item you can imagine, with a better variation in styles than in most shops. A similar, but less spectacular craft market operates nearby on Mere Puiestee, just north of Vana-Viru Street. In summer, temporary markets also spring up from week to week on or near Town Hall Square, where there's an enchanting month-long **Christmas Market**.

> **NOTES**
>
> Market vendors may give you a small discount for buying in volume, but generally they do not barter. The price they quote is what they expect to get.

An equally fascinating place to pick up a gift or two is **Katariina Guild**, in St Catherine's Passage (www.katariinagild.eu), which runs from the Sweater Wall to Vene Street. In this string of small workshops, visitors can watch craftspeople at work creating quilts, ceramics, glass items, jewellery, hats and hand-painted silk. While the artists use time-honoured methods, their products are usually modern, even avant-garde.

The more traditional Estonian handicrafts are available in any souvenir shop, but the most authentic and interesting are sold by **Eesti Käsitöö** (www.crafts.ee), which runs shops on Pikk 22 and Vanaturu kael 8. Here you can find everything from dolls and wooden toys to entire Estonian folk costumes.

Shoppers looking for everyday fashion and other non-souvenir items will find the best selection in large department stores and malls outside the Old Town. The most notable of these are the **Viru Centre** (http://virukeskus.com/en) and the attached **Kaubamaja** department store (www.kaubamaja.ee), both in central Tallinn next to Viru Square. Tallinn's branch of **Stockmann** (www.stockmann.ee), the esteemed Finnish department store, is a short walk from there at Liivalaia 53. Other good shopping centres, such as the **Kristiine Centre** (www.kristiinekeskus.ee) and the **Ülemiste Centre** (www.ulemiste.ee), can be reached by bus.

WHAT TO BUY

Handicrafts, in all shapes and forms, are still the undisputed rulers of the city's souvenir world, thanks to modern Estonia's strong connection to its rural past. **Knitted items**, such as woollen jumpers, mittens, gloves, socks and hats, top the wishlist. Most of the knitwear is created in typical Estonian or Nordic patterns. A particularly fun variation sold here is a ridiculously long woollen cap, the drooping end of which is supposed to be tied around the neck like a scarf. Almost as common as knitwear is **linen**, which has been produced here since medieval times. A huge variety of items is available, ranging from tablecloths to dresses.

Anything made of **carved wood**, particularly fragrant juniper, is also a popular Estonian souvenir. Toys, dolls, beer mugs, butter knives and countless other wooden handicrafts make excellent and inexpensive gifts.

Beaded jewellery made of amber

Though it actually comes from Lithuania and Poland, **amber** has become a pan-Baltic souvenir, and many visitors feel obliged to pick up at least one piece of amber jewellery when visiting Tallinn. Apart from its well-known caramel colour, it can also be found in white, green and deep brown.

Antiques of all sorts are widely sold throughout the Old Town. Antique furniture, gramophones and Russian icons are available, though buyers should be aware of

The ubiquitous Vana Tallinn liqueur

the restrictions on exporting items made before 1945 (see page 140). Even for non-collectors, browsing one of the low-end vintage shops can be an adventure as they are typically packed with unique **Soviet-era trinkets**.

Estonia has also become known for its **cutting-edge fashion** and **home decor**, with designers selling their offbeat creations from speciality boutiques around town. These items often have an arty, Nordic edge.

One souvenir that says 'Tallinn' like no other is **Vana Tallinn liqueur**, available from any alcohol-seller for a modest price. The sweet, dark liquid can be sipped as-is from a shot glass or, better still, added to coffee or ice cream. Bottles of Vana Tallinn are often sold in linen satchels, packaging them perfectly for gifts. Finally, just as sweet as the liqueur but far less hazardous are **chocolates**, either those made by Tallinn's famous Kalev confectionery company (www.kalev.eu), available in nicely decorated boxes, or the exquisite handmade chocolates sold in speciality cafés in the Old Town.

SPORTS AND OUTDOOR ACTIVITIES

As in most European countries, football is king among spectator sports. Both the national team and Tallinn's *Meistriliiga* (top-league) club FC Flora play their home games at A Le Coq Arena (Asula 4c; www.jalgpall.ee/ejl/a-le-coq-arena).

Basketball enjoys nearly equal popularity, with Tallinn's Kalev/Cramo the most recognised of the handful of teams based around the country. Both the Kalev/Cramo and the national team play their games at Unibet Arena (www.unibetarena.ee).

Fans who want to watch their home team's rugby or football match on satellite TV should head to Old Town pubs such as **Nimeta** (Suur-Karja 4) or **Beer Garden** (Inseneri 1; www.beergarden.ee), both of which have large screens and plenty of beer and snacks.

Swimming is possible year-round thanks to several indoor pools around the city. Among the most easily accessible is the pool at the *Kalev Spa Hotel & Water Park* (Aia 18; www.kalevspa.ee). In summer, however, **Pirita Beach** provides a decent, if crowded, place to get wet. The more adventurous can even try their hand at Estonia's favourite watersport – **windsurfing**. The Battery Pirita Surfclub (www.surf.ee) offers four-hour lessons for beginners, with equipment and wetsuits provided.

Tallinn's nearest **golf** centre is the Estonian Golf & Country Club (www.egcc.ee), about 25 minutes' drive from town,

> **NOTES**
>
> In Estonia, skiing is second nature. Every February thousands set out on the gruelling 63km (39-mile) Tartu Marathon (www.tartumaraton.ee). The cross-country race is part of the international Worldloppet series, and attracts competitors from around the world.

Windsurfing: Estonia's favourite watersport

which features an eighteen-hole course by the sea. **Tennis** clubs in Tallinn are also visitor-friendly. Good choices are the Rocca al Mare Tennis Centre (Haabersti 5; http://tenniseklubi.ee) and the Kalevi Tenniseklubi (Herne 28; www.kalevitenniseklubi.ee).

In winter, **ice skating** is a great choice for outdoor fun. At the Harju Ice Rink (www.uisuplats.ee), in the park along Harju Street, you can glide around to music while taking in the Old Town surroundings.

CHILDREN

Tallinn does not offer too many obvious activities for children, but with a little strategic planning, you should have no trouble keeping the smile on any young face.

The most fun way to tour the Old Town in summer is hitching a ride on the hop-on, hop-off CitySightseeing bus (www.

104 THINGS TO DO

citysightseeing.ee), which tours the historic centre and Old Town, Pirita and the suburbs. The **bicycle taxis** operating in the centre also provide an amusing option for getting around.

Among the main child-oriented attractions in Old Town is the **Estonian Theatre for Young Audiences and Museum of Puppetry Arts** (Lai 1, Nunne 4; www.eestinoorsooteater.ee), an extensive and high-tech display of the creatures created by the well-loved **Estonian Puppet Theatre**. Not far away, the fifteenth-century **Epping Tower** (Laboratooriumi 31; www.epping.ee) introduces the medieval era with several floors of hands-on exhibits. Here, young visitors are even invited to try on chain mail and armour.

For those with a sweet tooth, there's the **Kalev Chocolate Shop and Sweets Mastery** (Roseni 7; www.kalev.eu), which displays

An interactive wall at the NUKU Museum of Puppet Arts

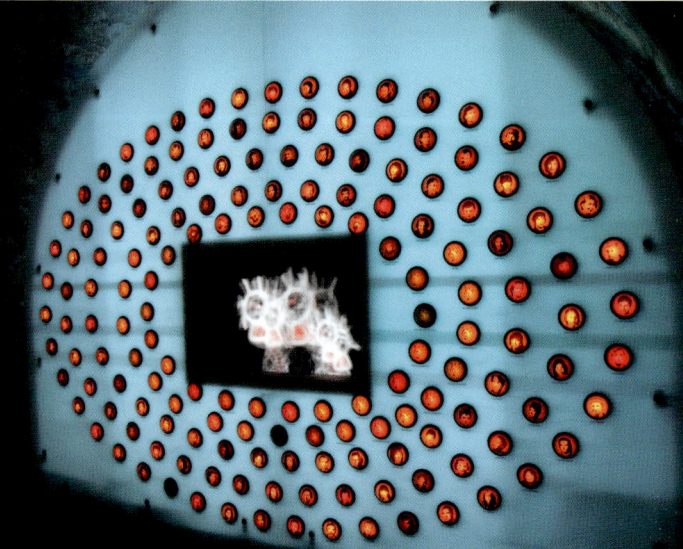

over two hundred marzipan creations and offers workshops on how to make the almond sweet and figurines.

Outside the medieval walls in Kadriorg Park, you'll find the small domed folly housing the **Children's Museum Miiamilla** (Koidula 21C; www.linnamuuseum.ee/lastemuuseum-miiamilla), packed with hands-on play-kitchens, faux shops and soft-play areas for babies and toddlers – plus a café serving mini-pancakes and juice. Aimed at children aged 3 to 11, it also has one of the city's best playgrounds, with a small amusement park and carousel beyond.

Farther out, the **Tallinn Zoo** (Paldiski mnt. 145; www.tallinnzoo.ee) never fails to enthral young visitors with its 350-plus species of animal – wolves, tigers, bears, elephants and lynx among them – though it can be a depressing sight with its small enclosures and less-than-optimal habitats. Older children will want to head out to the **FK Centre** (Paldiski mnt. 229a; www.fkkeskus.ee), where they can engage in a laser shoot-out or live out their Formula-1 fantasies on the high-speed, motorised go-cart track. **Pirita Beach** is a popular destination for family fun in the warm season, but no matter what time of year, kids can make a splash at the centrally located, indoor **Kalev Spa Water Park** (Aia 18; www.kalevspa.ee), which has water slides as well as bubble baths and kiddie pools.

FESTIVALS AND EVENTS

Tallinn hosts a number of festivals throughout the year, most of them centred on music and dance or designed to showcase the city's medieval past. In this extreme climate, events are carefully scheduled to take account of the season, though jazz and dance festivals and classical concert cycles might happen at any time of year. Visitors may also be interested in major festivals in nearby towns. Big draws are the **Pärnu Music Festival** in July (www.parnumusicfestival.tv/pmf) and the popular **Viljandi Folk Music Festival** (www.viljandifolk.ee), hosted in late July in the historic southern town of Viljandi.

Concert at the Old Town Days Festival

1 January New Year's fireworks on Freedom Square.
April Tallinn Music Week (https://tmw.ee): the nation's top musical acts showcase their talent. Jazzkaar (www.jazzkaar.ee/en): international jazz festival, featuring world-class performers from Estonia and abroad.
June Old Town Days Festival (http://vanalinnapaevad.ee): entertaining mix of medieval tournaments, markets and concerts all over the Old Town.
July OlleSummer (www.ollesummer.ee): the season's largest outdoor party. Four days of beer tasting and concerts by Estonia's top bands. Tallinn Maritime Days (www.tallinnamerepaevad.ee): a weekend of boat-themed family entertainment at the harbours.
July–August International Organ Festival (www.festivals.ee).
August Birgitta Festival (www.filharmoonia.ee/en/birgitta): a week-long modern musical theatre festival against the backdrop of the Pirita Convent ruins.
September–November Sõltumatu Tantsu Lava (www.stl.ee): three months of dance and activities at Telliskivi Creative City.
November Pöff (www.poff.ee): international feature films, with sub-festivals for student films, children's films and animation.
December Christmas Market in Town Hall Square (www.christmasmarket.ee). Advent concerts in churches throughout town.

Food and drink

During Estonia's post-independence renaissance, Tallinn established itself as a reliable destination for foodies, dedicated to fresh, local ingredients and traditional recipes honouring the nation's pre-Soviet days. Sustainable farming and natural, organic methods that kept Estonians fed during the lean years were passed down and eagerly adopted by younger generations uninhibited by the baggage of the twentieth century. In the past decade, Tallinn has matured with the confidence of a world-class city that's more Scandinavian than Baltic in many ways. Restaurants are competitive with their Western European counterparts. Many chefs have been internationally trained. And Michelin has taken notice, anointing new spots like *180° by Matthias Diether* and *NOA* with stars.

Even so, dining out in Tallinn is still a relative bargain. Here, a ten-course tasting menu on a heated terrace overlooking the beach can set diners back less than €80 a head. Order a sourdough pizza with artisanal cheese, and you'll receive change from a tenner. Local wines are more sophisticated than they ever have been, as newly moneyed Estonians invest in growing and making around the country. And French and Italian vintages are as affordable here as on a shelf in a Parisian supermarket.

Elk soup on the menu

Alfresco lunch on Viru Street

While Old Town still has the highest concentration of atmospheric restaurants, it also – not surprisingly – caters to a high concentration of tourists, especially when the weather heats up. Locals, meanwhile, have established, discovered and gentrified new corners of the city. The post-industrial harbour Port Noblessner, a burgeoning live-work-play district with a lively marina, attracts all sorts with its waterside terraces and outdoor sculptures – it buzzes from noon until midnight. Venturing to up-and-coming Kadriorg and Pirita is as gratifying on a wine-soaked evening out as during a day exploring the parks and museums.

TOP 10 THINGS TO TRY

1. MULGIPUDER
Most breakfast buffets include this savoury Estonian barley porridge, a traditional peasant dish modernised with bacon and a side of sourdough toast.

2. KILUVÕILEIB
Technically an open-faced sandwich topped with sprats, or herring, this rye-bread snack has spawned contemporary versions flecked with sliced veg, herbs and the obligatory boiled egg.

3. KRINGEL
Inspired by Danish and Swedish baked goods, this twisted pastry is spiked with cardamom, cinnamon or saffron; increasingly, it is filled with delicacies like truffle and cheese.

4. PIRUKAS
Like savoury kringels, these rye-flower braids traditionally conceal a fish and cabbage filling but today are often baked with vegetarian fillings like carrot and onion.

5. KÜPSETATUD ÕUNAD
In autumn, you'll be digging into one of these baked apples studded with raisins and nuts and dusted with cinnamon.

Pavement restaurants in the Old Town

6. ROSOLJE
Try this side salad of purple cabbage, beetroot, boiled potato and optional herring with your *kiluvõileib* (above).

7. ADZIKA
If your tastes run spicier than the mild Baltic culinary traditions, add a splash of this piquant sauce to your plate.

8. KVASS
Popular throughout Eastern Europe, this fermented rye beverage has a cloudy appearance and a yeasty, beer-like tang.

9. VANA TALLINN
Undeniably Estonian, this punchy liqueur has a Jamaican rum base infused with sweet caramel tones and citrusy top notes. It's usually served on ice with a lemon wedge

10. PELMENI
Most traditional restaurants will serve these Russian dumplings stuffed with beef and pork, or duck and thyme, accompanied with yoghurt sauce for dipping.

WHERE TO EAT

Before the global Covid-19 pandemic, most visitors to Tallinn were content to dine within the confines of the Old Town and its city centre neighbours. But as the focus of daily life shifted into more residential suburbs, and post-industrial Tallinn reinvented itself, restaurants began popping up to capture the footfall. Today you'll find smart, sophisticated, accessible restaurants in residential and seaside enclaves that were once foodie wastelands.

Kadriorg is a viable option after dark, right out to the beaches of Pirita. And in the western corner of the city, Telliskivi, Kalamaja and the new Port Noblessner marina development have cultivated a

Herring on dark bread – the Estonian national sandwich

range of low- to high-brow restaurants and cafés. Trams and buses will whisk you across town in under half an hour, wherever you are, and ride-shares with Bolt and Uber are always available through the apps. Keep in mind: it's best to book ahead even at a casual haunt, or you risk being turned away. And it's fairly common for the host to assign you a time slot of two or three hours at posher restaurants.

Breakfast is typically served until 10am on weekdays and noon at weekends. An excellent alternative to the hotel breakfast is the beloved *pagariäri*, or bakery. These are usually open by 9am, and serve fresh pastries, cakes, coffee and tea. Try **Café Värav** (Väike Rannavärav 4; www.facebook.com/varavcafe), **Røst Bakery** (Rotermanni 14; www.rost.ee) or the excellent **Bekker Pagariäri** (Kopli tn 27; www.bakery.ee) in the Kopli neighbourhood. The town's oldest bakery-café, **Maiasmokk** (Pikk 16; www.kohvikmaiasmokk.

ee), is worth visiting for its old-fashioned wood decor, the tempting, aromatic baked goods and handmade chocolate pralines.

Dinner crowds fill Tallinn's restaurants between 6.30 and 9pm on weekdays, shifting an hour or two later on Friday and Saturday evenings. Late diners should note that most restaurants stop serving food around 10 or 11pm, but some pubs in Old Town will keep their kitchens open until midnight.

VEGETARIANS

Though the idea of anyone willingly giving up meat is baffling to many pork-chop-loving Estonians, Tallinn has more vegetarian restaurants today than ever before. One of the most popular is **Vegan Restoran V** (Rataskaevu tn 12; www.veganrestoran.ee/en) in Old Town, which serves a fine beetroot ravioli and excellent vegetarian risottos and plant-based burgers. Catering as they do to the international market, many restaurants in Old Town have added *taimetoidud*, or vegetarian, dishes to their menus. You'll often find potato pancakes and stews along with the usual vegetable stir-fries. If you plan to order a soup or salad that appears to be

ETIQUETTE

Estonian menus have a few nuances that can be confusing to foreigners. For instance, when ordering, it's important to keep in mind that a 'salad' may turn out to be a mixture of finely chopped meat, rice, potatoes or vegetables mixed with mayonnaise and served in a small side dish. A 'sandwich' is usually open-faced: a single, small slice of bread topped with a simple piece of cheese, meat or fish. Pancakes, or *pannkoogid*, are not primarily served as a breakfast food. Thick pancakes with savoury fillings such as ham and cheese, tuna, mushrooms and prawns are often offered as a snack or a main course at lunch, while honey- or jam-filled pancakes make popular desserts. Similarly, omelettes can just as readily be available for lunch and dinner as they can for breakfast.

Tallinn's Beer House serves up seven varieties of house brew

meat-free from the menu description, confirm with your server: it's common for recipes to contain bits of ham.

TO HELP YOU ORDER...
Could we have a table? **Palun kas me saaksime laua?**
I'd like a/an/some… **Ma sooviksin…**
The bill, please. **Palun arvet**

bread (dark) **leib**
bread (light) **sai**
butter **või**
coffee **kohv**
dessert **dessert/magustoit**
fish **kala**
fruit **puuvili**
ice cream **jäätis**
meat **liha**
menu **menüü**
milk **piim**
pepper **pipar**
potatoes **kartulid**
rice **riis**

FOOD AND DRINK

> **NOTES**
>
> Having a drink with a local? When toasting, Estonians clink their glasses and say 'Terviseks!' ('to your health'). And as your glasses touch, it is absolutely vital to make eye-to-eye contact with each person.

eelroad starters
forell trout
hapukapsas sauerkraut
jäätis ice cream
juust cheese
kala fish
kalkun turkey
kana chicken
kartulid potatoes
kaste sauce
koha pike
kohv coffee
köögiviljad vegetables
koor cream
krevetid prawn
kurk cucumber
lasteroad children's menu
leib dark bread
liha meat
lisandid side orders
lõhe salmon
magustoi-dud desserts
õlu beer

salad **salat**
salt **sool**
sandwich **võileib**
soup **supp**
tea **tee**
wine **vein**
vegetarian **taimetoitlane**

...AND READ THE MENU

omletid omelettes
pannkoogid pancakes
pardiliha duck
piim milk
porgand carrot
praed main courses
riis rice
sai white bread
salatid salads
sealiha pork
seened mushrooms
sink ham
supid soups
suupisted appetisers
taimetoi-dud vegetarian dishes
tee tea
tomat tomato
tuunikala tuna
vein wine
veiseliha beef
viin vodka
vesi water

Places to eat

The price categories below are based on the average cost of a three-course meal for one person, and do not include drinks or tip.

€€€€ = over €45
€€€ = €35–€45
€€ = €25–€35
€ = under €25

OLD TOWN

Beer House Dunkri 5; www.beerhouse.ee. A lively venue on any given weekend, this vast, German-style beer hall is the place to go for hulking portions of meat and sausage. True to its name, it serves up seven varieties of house brew. Be sure to check out the inventive back 'courtyard' and brace yourself for tourist-oriented Bavarian bands at night. €€€

Botaanik Suurtüki 2; www.botaanik.ee. A hole-in-the-wall speakeasy with an emphasis on cocktails, the 'Botanist' riffs on the classics: think 'spring gimlet' infused with berries and a wintertime 'cranberry sour'. The sweet, savvy staff recommend booking by email well in advance to secure one of the few tables. If you're a fan of caviar, you can order it here at a price far cheaper than anywhere in the UK. Reservations required. €€€

Controvento Vene 12; www.controvento.ee. Consistently high-quality Italian cuisine and professional service has made *Controvento* a long-time favourite of Tallinn's expatriate community – it's the oldest Italian in the city, in fact. The setting – a cosy medieval building in the Katariina passageway encourages groups to linger for hours, ordering course after course from *bruschetta* to *tiramisu*. Reservations at weekends are essential. €€€

Elevant Vene 5; www.elevant.ee. One of Old Town's most amusing restaurants, this beloved Indian has assimilated slightly with an Estonian-inspired 'wild menu' that features items such as moose and wild salmon curries. A long list of traditional curries, biriyanis and masalas also satisfy in this charming dining room staffed with enthusiastic young servers. €€€

Gloria Müürivahe 2; www.gloria.ee. *Gloria* is the sort of place people book when they truly want to spoil themselves. The restaurant, which opened in 1937, has hosted a number of statespeople and dignitaries, including Pope John Paul II and Lech Walesa. The interior is a study in prewar decadence – antiques, potted palms and private booths closed off by velvet curtains. An interesting mix of French, Italian, Baltic and Russian creations makes up the menu. Anyone who wants to taste a bit of *Gloria*'s glory without committing to a full meal can visit its attractive wine cellar. €€€€

Kaerajaan Raekoja plats 17; www.kaerajaan.ee. For an inventive spin on Estonian ingredients – and brilliant displays of folk patterns – head to this vibrant restaurant overlooking Town Hall Square. Both the colourful ground-floor café and the more formal upper floors display fun-loving decor. The food, while flirting with traditionally Estonian flavours, will be recognisable to global tastes and more than satisfy. €€€

Kohvik Must Puudel Müürivahe 20; www.facebook.com/MustPuudel. A trip back in time to the Soviet 1980s – thankfully extending only to the interior decor – has made the 'Black Poodle' a favourite among young locals, many of whom crowd in late at night for wine and laughs. Genuine, junky remnants of the era have been cleverly arranged to create a casual atmosphere that is rounded out by quite decent, inexpensive food and cheerful service. €€

Kompressor Rataskaevu 3; www.kompressorpub.ee. This popular student haunt – locals call it a pub – is a budget traveller's dream. There are a handful of soups, salads and snacks on the menu, but what draws a crowd is its comprehensive list of sweet and savoury pancakes: filled with smoked chicken, pepperoni, turkey, prawns and feta. One portion is a meal in itself and, at around €8, a true bargain. Be prepared to wait. €€

Lee Restoran Uus 31; www.leeresto.ee. Estonian for the communal fireplace crucial to family life, *Lee* makes high-quality modern dishes, like trout sashimi and grass-fed beef tenderloin, seem like a homely kitchen supper. It even does a (reasonably priced) 'family dinner' with six large sharing plates for the whole table. Reservations recommended. €€€

Olde Hansa Vana turg 1; www.oldehansa.ee. This medieval-style restaurant in the heart of the Old Town may appear touristy from the outside, but once you're served you'll understand why a visit to Tallinn would not be complete without experiencing *Olde Hansa*. Far more intricate and authentic than a typical theme restaurant, it offers a fascinating menu and a truly Hanseatic atmosphere, complete with costumed waitresses, candlelight and minstrels. Reserve at weekends. €€€

Peet Ruut Rataskaevu 8; www.peetruut.com. A simple, humble dining room for simple, humble fare with an Asian bent, this newcomer on a pretty, cobbled street epitomises nu-Estonian dining. The wines are natural, the produce and proteins are mostly organic and local, and the dishes make the most of just a few ingredients. The menu changes regularly but always features more vegetarian options than most. Having taken over one of Tallinn's top dining establishments and become equally popular itself, the restaurant highly recommends making reservations. €€€€

Peppersack Viru 2/Vana turg 6; www.peppersack.ee. Not quite the medieval experience one might expect when looking from the outside, *Peppersack* is nevertheless worth a visit for its historic interior and friendly service – and medieval-sized hunks of meat still arrive with the steak knife jammed in (and a mug of beer, if you're up for it). Try the beer-steeped lamb stew and stay for an order of apple pancakes with cream. With the tourist very much in mind, *Peppersack* stages jousting and bellydancing on weekends. €€€

Rado Vene 7; www.radorestoran.ee. Like many a French bistro, a new menu appears daily on the blackboard. Yet here, the bulk of ingredients are simply what chef Rado Mitro can get his hands on that day. Roasted veg in creamy sauces, seafood pastas and local duck breast with courgette flowers are artfully plated with real flowers and delivered by Mitro's partner and sommelier, Triinu. Summer-fruit tarts with home-made ice cream are worth saving up for, and saving room for. Reservations required. **€€€€**

Tchaikovsky Vene 9 (Hotel Telegraaf); www.telegraafhotel.com/et/restoran-tallinnas. Advertised as a 'symphony of Russian cuisine', this is one of Estonia's top restaurants. Blending French tastes, Russian traditions and Estonian ingredients, it has an opulent nineteenth-century interior and a classy menu featuring delicacies from bluefin tuna tartare to borscht. The €98 multi-course menu is great value compared to Western European prices. **€€€€**

Troika Raekoja plats 15; www.troika.ee. The look resembles something straight out of a nineteenth-century Russian storybook, but don't let that put you off. This lavishly decorated cellar restaurant pours heart and soul into its Russian menu, dominated as much by familiar snacks like blini with cherries and lamb *barašek* dumplings as hearty, hard-hitting fare like Tver mutton and bear stroganoff. Its Town Hall Square location means *Troika* will be bustling most times of day, but the staff will have you sitting and served in good time. Plus thanks to the long opening hours, it's the best place for a late-night Baltic charcuterie board. Reservations encouraged. **€€**

Väike-rataskaevu Niguliste 6; www.rataskaevu16.ee. The smaller, more intimate sibling of Tallinn's popular *Rataskaevu 16*, this stone-and-log dining room elevates the usual meaty menu with fall-off-the-bone ribs, salty smoked-eel rösti and a memorable braised-elk roast with blackcurrant sauce, along with a few concessions to the weak at heart (or vegetarian). The wine list gives you more than what you pay for. Reservations encouraged. **€€€€**

KALAMAJA

Boheem Kopli 18; www.boheem.ee. The laid-back bohemian spirit of the Kalamaja neighbourhood is typified by this pleasant café, often packed with students in ironic eyeglasses and bulky scarves, discussing Sartre. Ideal for a light lunch or brunch, it specialises in meals like green salads, pancakes, wraps and platters of pickled veg. Prices are extremely reasonable. €€

F-Hoone Telliskivi 60a; tel: 5322 6855. Cleverly built into a former factory space of Telliskivi Creative City, *F-Hoone* is edgy in the way new-generation Tallinners have come to love. It operates as a restaurant by day, serving inexpensive meals, and turns into a bar and club on weekend nights. Find it by crossing to the back of the train station, heading east down Kopli and turning left at the first tram stop. €€

Põhjala Brewery & Tap Room Peetri 5; www.pohjalabeer.com. Põhjala brings America to the rejuvenated streets of Kalamaja. Its soaring industrial interior, updated with wrought iron, stainless steel and deconstructed pendant lights, is right out of Brooklyn and its menu of slow-cooked ribs and chicken roasts transports you to Texas. Vegans get burgers, fries and tangy grilled watermelon, but the thing here is the beer on tap, brewed, stored and sold in cans around back. Its new Põhjala Kõu lager with berries and honey is a summer treat. A book-ahead sauna accommodates up to eight people. €€€

CITY CENTRE, KADRIORG AND PIRITA

Horisont Tornimae Street 3; www.horisontrestoran.ee. The top floor of the *Swissôtel* is given over a five-star restaurant with five-star views of the city. If you can't score a window table, ask for a seat at the central bar and order the set menu, a breezy flavour journey for under €90 that includes two seafood starters and a lamb or vegetarian main, plus one of the one of the region's trademark fruit puddings. Reservations encouraged. €€€€

NOA Ranna 3; www.nch.ee. You have a choice of two tiers at *NOA*. The Michelin-starred tasting menu is a four-hour affair of larger-than-average marine-inspired dishes. The more affordable, more accessible menu spans continents and genres with hoisin-duck tacos, schnitzel, octopus pasta and miso black cod. Both are enjoyed behind a mile of sea-facing glass or on the expansive terrace. Absolutely worth the taxi out to the edge of the city. Reservations required. **€€€€**

NOP Köleri 1; www.nop.ee. A pretty clapboard café on a traditional street near Kadriorg Park, *NOP* scores a 'yep' from local families and remote workers looking for a natural boost in the afternoon. The chalkboard menu is dominated by earthy, healthy Vietnamese salads and sandwiches. Custardy puddings, rolls and fruit-dotted pastries hit the spot at teatime. And you can get a smoothie (and a kimchi *latke*) alongside your morning eggs. Come early when it's warm for a table on the courtyard terrace. **€€**

Platz Roseni 7; www.platz.ee. This cosy, brick-lined restaurant at the heart of the Rotermann Quarter has garnered a reputation for consistently serving up great contemporary cuisine. The menu is concise, a fusion of Asian and European tastes with plenty of options for vegetarians and pescatarians. What the chefs find fresh that day, they prepare lovingly and beautifully. There are few better spots for a summertime lunch than the east-facing terrace. **€€€**

Rataskaevu 16 16 Rataskaevu; http://rataskaevu16.ee. Foodies still flock to this highly rated traditional haunt for fine Estonian delicacies, including its famous fried herring fillets or elk roast. Vegetarians will also find plenty of options here. In summer, choose a table on the wonderful patio. **€€€€**

Restoran Salt Vase 14; www.saltrestoran.ee. *Salt* updates Nordic fusion cuisine with an inventive Estonian twist, presenting a careful, seasonal offering of fish and greens with an emphasis on the nation's favourite flavour-enhancer (clue's in the name). Mussels sit in a spicy coconut sauce; pan-fried fillet of sole is bathed in a summery salsa verde. Reservations required. €€€

Tar Tar Köök Bar Narva mnt. 7; tel: 6109 230. This bustling brasserie slightly east of centre has a loyal lunch crowd that goes for reasonably priced Estonian staples like *selyanka* (a hearty, smoky meat soup). Sandwiches and charcuterie platters are popular too. €€€€

Tuljak Pirita tee 26e; www.tuljak.ee. Watch the ferries head out into Tallinn Bay from one of the prettiest dining rooms in the city. A rare Modernist pavilion from the Soviet era, *Tuljak* was designed by Valve Pormeister, a rare female Modernist architect, in 1964. It served as a restaurant for decades but the current incarnation – restored and overhauled a decade ago – improved the views and the public landscaping that makes them so green. It gets rave reviews for its seafood – the freshest oysters, caviar and herring – but many come for its menu of spritzes and sparkling wines, perfect for sundowners. Reservations encouraged. €€€€

PORT NOBLESSNER

180° by Matthias Diether Staapli 4; www.180degrees.ee. Estonia's first chef with two Michelin stars is German-born Matthias Diether, who plays with French classics to deliver culinary artworks that can't be described in the five words or less the menu allows. It's better to be surprised anyway, by the delicate bracket of lobster steeped in bouillabaisse and dusted with paprika or the 'tomato marshmallow' sitting on a pillow of Comté. The set menu comes in just under a cool €200. Spending the evening in this soothing amber-lit dining room overlooking the bay is priceless. Reservations required. €€€€

KotKot Tallinn Noblessner Peetri 12; www.kotkot.world. This much-loved fast-food haunt grew out of a small street food pop-up created by the Michelin-awarded chef Kim Mikkola. The chicken burger is legendary in these parts; and its plant-based alternative is almost indistinguishable from the real deal. €

Lessner Peetri 12; www.lessner.ee. *Lessner*'s main calling card is sunset vibes, so the concrete, candlelit cavern doesn't even open until dinner time. It's also one of the city's most reliable late-night spots for a Pisco spritz or 'Tallinn negroni'. In summer you can spend hours nibbling on soft-shell crab with apple-mint salad, watching the sky change colour, and still have two hours before last call. €€€

Lore Bistroo Peetri 12; www.lorebistroo.ee. A veteran of Lee (see page 117) opened this marina-side gem to showcase fine Estonian produce in small, colourful combinations – like fresh squid tentacles with carrots and capers, or Järveotsa quail with broccoli and fragrant chimichurri sauce. The menu lists as many vegetarian options as the city's strictly vegan restaurants. Come to while away an afternoon watching the sailboats bob up ahead. €€€

KOPLI

Barbarea Marati 5; www.barbarea.ee. The biggest bargain in Tallinn is the €50 six-course set menu at this bar and kitchen in a rehabilitated warehouse district near Paddock Bay in the Kopli neighbourhood. Reserve a table in the front window and you'll watch farmers haul in bushels of morels and Romanesco broccoli to sauté alongside charred octopus or grass-fed entrecôte. True to its trendy feel, it serves dinner family-style, with chunks of home-baked bread and dips for sharing…and natural wines, naturally. Reservations required. €€€

Karjase Sai Bakery Marati 5; www.karjasesai.ee. As local a bakery as you'll find in Tallinn, *Karjase* sees queues forming before its 8am opening time, after which hipsters loiter around the former Põhjala factory building, sipping at lattes and picking at cardamom monkey bread. Bakers twist and plait in the background until after lunch. €€

Travel essentials

PRACTICAL INFORMATION

Accessible travel	**124**
Accommodation	**124**
Airport	**125**
Apps	**126**
Bicycle hire	**126**
Budgeting for your trip	**126**
Car hire	**127**
Climate	**128**
Crime and safety	**128**
Driving	**129**
Electricity	**130**
Embassies and consulates	**130**
Emergencies	**131**
Getting to Tallinn	**131**
Guides and tours	**131**
Health and medical care	**132**
Language	**133**
LGBTQ+ travellers	**134**
Media	**134**
Money	**134**
Opening times	**135**
Police	**136**
Post office	**136**
Public holidays	**137**
Telephones	**137**
Time zones	**137**
Tipping	**138**
Toilets	**138**
Tourist information	**138**
Transport	**139**
Visa and entry requirements	**140**
Websites and internet	**141**
Youth hostels	**141**

ACCESSIBLE TRAVEL

The medieval city centre is a headache for anyone in a wheelchair. Pavements can be rocky, kerbs steep, and many restaurants, cafés, shops and museums can only be accessed via cramped, narrow staircases. On the positive side, traffic is restricted, leaving streets wide open for pedestrian explorers. Although the situation has recently improved as Estonia is bound to meet EU regulations, visitors in wheelchairs will sometimes need to ask numerous, pointed and direct questions about a hotel's facilities to ensure they can be accommodated. The largest and newest hotels are fairly accessible, and almost always have rooms specially equipped for disabled guests. All new buildings and principal museums are equipped with accessible facilities. The number of buses, trams and trolleybuses with essential equipment to aid in boarding is growing, the major taxi companies also offer cars designed for disabled passengers.

ACCOMMODATION

Hotels in the centre of Tallinn historically came in two varieties: small, stylish, exclusive establishments within the Old Town, and large, towering, chain-type hotels just outside the Old Town. These are now being joined by spa hotels and mid-range boutique options in the city centre. Prices can vary substantially, so comparison-shopping is always a good idea. Many hotels offer discounts online. Bargain hunters should also note that rates for equivalent hotels located a short distance from the centre can be substantially lower.

Bargains can be snagged through Airbnb by following the 'guest favourite' tags in its search engine. This is where you'll find the most variety in terms of architecture, location and style, like a three-bed yacht at the Lennusadam marina, or a shingled eco-hut steps from the bay in Kalamaja.

For travellers staying three nights or more, renting a serviced flat is an alternative worth considering. Prices per night become cheaper the longer you stay. Family-run guesthouses and a few Soviet-era dormitories that have been turned into hotels provide cheap accommodation on Tallinn's periphery. For apartment rentals, check www.apartment.ee.

In all cases, booking well in advance is recommended. The best resource for vetted accommodation information is the Tallinn Tourism Office's extensive website (www.visittallinn.ee).

> I've a reservation. **Mul on tuba broneeritud.**
> I'd like a single/double room with a bath/shower.
> **Ma sooviksin ühelist/kahelist tuba vanniga/duššiga.**

AIRPORT

Tallinn Airport (www.airport.ee) is incredibly close to Kadriorg and the city centre. Arrival and departure areas are located in two halves of the same long hall. As you enter the arrival area after baggage claim, ATMs and banks are to your left, towards the centre of the hall. An information desk just beyond them only provides details on the airport itself and how to get into town. Car-hire companies are downstairs.

Taxis wait just outside the arrivals area's main door, straight ahead. An airport transfer by taxi can take as little as ten minutes and the fare should be around €15. Ride shares can be arranged through the Bolt app (www.bolt.eu). Bus stops are located on the lower concourse, one escalator flight down from the arrivals hall. Buses to the centre depart from stop No. 1. City bus No. 2, which will take you to a stop next to the Viru shopping mall in the centre, departs from the airport every twenty to thirty minutes. Its timetable is posted next to the stop. The ten-minute journey costs €2. Pay the driver as you board. You can also take tram route 4, which takes you to the city centre in around fifteen minutes for €2.

> What bus do I take to the centre? **Missugune buss sõidab kesklinna?**
> How much is the fare to…? **Kui palju maksab pilet…?**
> Will you tell me when to get off? **Palun öelge kus ma pean väljuma?**

APPS

The typically Estonian high-tech approach to modern life is also applied to concerns about the environment and sustainability. If you need to visit places that are not easily accessible via public transport, a variety of useful car-sharing apps, like CityBee (https://citybee.lt), have been developed to keep people mobile while reducing the number of private vehicles on the roads. It can also be used to access electric cars and scooters.

BICYCLE HIRE

Getting around by bicycle is a perfect way to explore the leafy Kadriorg district, Pirita Beach area and the shoreline that stretches between them.

City Bike (www.citybike.ee) hires out bikes for periods ranging from one hour (€3) to a day (€12) or a week (€50). The price includes safety equipment and locks. The firm can deliver and pick up bicycles from other locations.

BUDGETING FOR YOUR TRIP

Prices in Tallinn are generally cheaper than in other European capitals, particularly for food and drink. Those planning to do extensive sightseeing should consider picking up the city's discount card, the **Tallinn Card**, available in 24hr, 48hr and 72hr versions at €43, €63 and €76, respectively. The card gives holders free access to over fifty attractions and museums, free use of public transport (plus hop-on, hop-off buses), and discounts in a number of shops and restaurants, as well as reduced prices of sightseeing tours. Consider carefully before buying one on a Monday or Tuesday, when many museums are closed. Cards can be downloaded onto a smartphone or purchased in person at a Tourist Information Centre (see page 138) or at larger hotels.

Accommodation. Youth hostel travellers can find beds for about €17, though most are in the €20–€40 range. A budget hotel with an en-suite room will be €50–€80, whereas high-end establishments will charge €100 and up.

Buses and trams. Single-ride tickets purchased from the driver cost €2, a 1hr e-ticket (smartcard) validation costs €2 and an all-day ticket costs

€5.50. A smartcard, which can be bought at any R-Kiosk, post office or government office, can be used for a group of up to six people.

Entertainment. Mid-range tickets to a symphony concert average €25, cinema tickets at weekends cost €8, and entrance to a popular nightclub costs €10 to €15.

Food and drink. A light lunch, without drinks, can be had for between €12 and €15 per person, whereas an average three-course evening meal will run to €35 or €40. A large beer in a local pub costs €5, and in a touristy café, €7. Soft drinks are usually priced at about €2.50.

Museums. Museum tickets for adults usually cost between €5 and €15.

CAR HIRE

Unless you plan to travel around the countryside during your stay, there's no real need to hire a car when visiting Tallinn. Nearly all the important sites are within easy walking distance of one another; the rest can be reached with a short tram or bus ride.

Most major international car-hire agencies operate in the city. All have rental desks on the lower floor of Tallinn Airport, and some also have offices in the city centre.

To hire a car, a driver must be at least 21 years of age, possess a valid driving licence with photo, and must have held a licence for at least two years.

Avis: at the airport and in the city; www.avis.ee.
Budget: at the airport; www.budget.ee.
Hertz: at the airport and in the city; www.hertz.ee.
R-Rent: at the airport; www.rrent.ee.
Sir Rent: in the city; www.sirrent.ee.
Sixt: at the airport and in the city; www.sixt.ee.

I'd like to hire a car. **Ma sooviksin üürida autot.**
I'd like it for a day/week. **Ma sooviksin seda üheks päevaks nädalaks.**
Where's the nearest petrol station? **Kus on lähim bensiinijaam?**

CLIMATE

Winter days can be either bitterly cold or uncomfortably damp. Spring and autumn are unpredictable, with temperatures hovering just above freezing. The best time to visit is unquestionably summer, when the weather is mildest and the northern skies stay light until after 11pm, although June and July are also the wettest months, and can bring heavy rain showers. The following chart shows the average monthly highs and lows in Tallinn:

	J	F	M	A	M	J	J	A	S	O	N	D
°C	0	-1	2	9	13	19	22	20	15	10	3	0
	5	-7	-5	0	3	9	11	10	6	3	-1	-5
°F	32	29	36	49	56	66	71	69	60	50	38	31
	22	17	22	32	38	48	53	51	43	38	29	22

CRIME AND SAFETY

Your chances of becoming the victim of a crime are remote, but the city is not crime-free. The most common offences against foreigners involve mugging and petty theft, an activity that is concentrated on Old Town's Viru Street. Take care that your wallet isn't temptingly jutting from your pocket, and that your bag or mobile phone is not sitting too close to the outer rail of the café. Leave valuables in your hotel, preferably in the safe, and keep your car in a guarded car park at night.

Violent crime against foreigners is rare, but you can use common sense to reduce the risk. Avoid unfamiliar, unlit areas at night, particularly if you're alone. Drink responsibly, and don't end up stumbling out of a pub late at night with a group of strangers. If you fall victim to a crime, call the general emergency number: 112 or the Municipal Police Department (tel: 661 9860).

> Call the police. **Kutsuge politsei.**
> My handbag/wallet has been stolen. **Minu käekoti/rahakoti on ära varastatud.**

Stop thief! **Peatage varas!**
Help! **Appi!**
Leave me alone! **Jätke mind rahule!**

DRIVING

Road conditions. Road conditions in Estonia are generally good, both in Tallinn and on motorways. The biggest hazard is usually other drivers, whose habits range from the careless to the aggressive. Your only recourse is to drive defensively. Weather is the next issue, particularly in winter when patches of ice appear on streets and roads. If you don't know how to drive in winter conditions, this is not the place to learn. Also, because markings on rural routes can often be confusing, a GPS-enabled map is essential. Finally, drivers unfamiliar with Tallinn should avoid Old Town, with its confusing one-way system.

Road signs. Traffic signs and symbols in Estonia follow the European standard.

Rules and regulations. Drive on the right and overtake on the left. Estonian law requires that headlights be kept on at all times, day and night, even in the city. The basic speed limit outside built-up areas is 90km/h (56mph), in built-up areas 50km/h (31mph), and in residential areas 20km/h (13mph). Some roads are marked with their own limits, particularly large motorways, where cars are permitted to travel at 110km/h (69mph) in summer. In the city, passengers in both front seats must wear seatbelts at all times. On motorways, the same rule applies to back-seat passengers as well. Children under 12 are not allowed in the front seat. Winter tyres must be used from 1 December to 1 March, though the dates can change from year to year. Valid foreign driving licences can be used in Estonia for up to a year; no international licence is needed.

Filling up. First pump, then pay. Fuel comes in four varieties: 92, 95, 98 and diesel. Most drivers use the 95 or the higher-quality 98. A litre of fuel generally costs around €1.70.

Parking. Finding street parking in Tallinn's busy centre can be a true test of will. Most is paid parking, but the first fifteen minutes is free (except in private car parks). Tickets are sold in vending machines or via mobile apps for between €1 and €8 per hour, depending on the area. Car parks/garages may be an easier option in central Tallinn. These can be found under Freedom Square (Vabaduse väljak), on Rävala 5, and in the Viru Centre (Viru Väljak 4/6). The cost is typically €2.20 for thirty minutes. For details on parking in Tallinn, visit www.parkimine.ee.

If you need help. Dial 118 for road service. They will tow your car to the nearest garage. If you need police or an ambulance, dial 112.

> Are we on the right road for…? **Kas me oleme õigel teel…?**
> Fill the tank, please with 92/95/98/diesel. **Palun täitke paak 92/95/98/diisel.**
> My car has broken down. **Mu auto läks katki.**
> There's been an accident. **Juhtus õnnetus.**

ELECTRICITY

The electricity in Estonia is 220 volts AC, 50Hz. Plugs are the round, two-pinned variety used in continental Europe, and adaptors can be found in electronic shops and in department stores.

EMBASSIES AND CONSULATES

Note that some embassies that serve Estonia are not in Estonia.

Australia. Klarabergsviadukten 63, 8th fl. 111 64 Stockholm, Sweden; tel: (+46 8) 613 29 00; www.sweden.embassy.gov.au.

Canada. Toomkooli 13, Tallinn; tel: 6273 311; www.estonia.gc.ca.

Ireland. Alberta Street 13, Riga, Latvia; (371) 6703 9370; www.embassyofireland.ee.

South Africa. 4th fl., Fleminggaten 20, Stockholm, Sweden; tel: (+46) 824 3950; www.visahq.com/south-africa/embassy/latvia.

UK. Wismari 6, Tallinn; tel: 6674 700; www.gov.uk/world/organisations/british-embassy-tallinn.

US. Kentmanni 20, Tallinn; tel: 6688 100; https://ee.usembassy.gov.

> Where is the British/American Embassy? **Kus on Inglise/ Ameerika saatkond?**

EMERGENCIES
Police, fire, paramedics: 112

> Where can I find a doctor who speaks English? **Kust ma vôiksin leida arsti, kes räägib inglise keelt?**

GETTING TO TALLINN
From the UK. British Airways (www.britishairways.com) and the budget airlines easyJet (www.easyjet.com; flying from Gatwick), Ryanair (www.ryanair.com; from Stansted) and Wizz Air (www.wizzair.com; from Luton) all operate direct flights between London and Tallinn, as does the Latvian low-cost airline airBaltic (www.airbaltic.com; from Gatwick). Other airlines, such as SAS (www.scandinavian.net) and Finnair (www.finnair.com), offer flights that connect through Stockholm and Helsinki, respectively, though these routes are usually more expensive.

From outside Europe. There are two basic strategies: nab the best deal you can on a flight to London, then take an easyJet, Ryanair or airBaltic flight (see above), or use one of the airlines that can connect you to Tallinn through its regional hub. The major airlines with services to Tallinn are airBaltic, Finnair, SAS, Lufthansa and LOT Polish Airways.

From neighbouring countries. If you are travelling from elsewhere in the Baltics or Central Europe, the bus, not the train, is the way to go. Eurolines (www.eurolines.com) offers frequent connections and good rates. From the north, overnight ferries make a slow connection from Stockholm, and each day dozens of ships ply the quick 85km (53-mile) crossing from Helsinki.

GUIDES AND TOURS
A wide range of intriguing city tours is available, from self-guided audio-tours

to offbeat, themed group walks. Tourist Information (see page 138) provides a complete list and can also put you in touch with a private guide. Among the more popular tours is the **Hop-on Hop-Off City Tour** (www.citytour.ee), which runs open-top buses on three regular routes. For a well-rounded, standard orientation, try the **Tallinn Official Sightseeing Tour** by Reisiekspert (https://travel-expert.eu). The combination bus and walking tour covers all the city's major sights. Another option is the **Welcome to Tallinn guided bicycle tour** organised by City Bike (www.citybike.ee). The more adventurous can try the **Sea Kayak Tour** run by 360 (www.360.ee), which lets visitors paddle out into the bay for a different view of the medieval skyline. No experience is required. Meanwhile, **Tallinn Traveller** (www.traveller.ee) offers several walking and bike tours, as well as daily trips from Tallinn.

> Is there an English-speaking guide? **Kas teil on inglise keelt kõnelev giid?**
> Can you translate this for me? **Kas te oskate seda mulle tõlkida?**

HEALTH AND MEDICAL CARE

Visiting Estonia poses no significant health risks and there are no issues with water quality. One concern, however, which only applies to visitors who spend time deep in the Estonian wilderness, is tick-borne encephalitis. If you plan to explore a forested area, you should arrange a vaccination before leaving home.

Western-produced medicines, including many of the same brands you would find at home, are widely available from any pharmacy *(apteek)*. Staff in central locations generally speak English, but selection is limited, so if you need a very specialised product, it is best to bring it with you. The **Südameapteek** (Tõnismägi 5; www.sudameapteek.ee) runs an all-night pharmacy window.

Estonia's healthcare system provides free emergency assistance to all visitors, and those who hold the European Health Insurance Card (EHIC) or Global Health Insurance Card (GHIC) are entitled to the same services as locals. However, it is still advisable to arrange a travel insurance policy that includes medical care before your trip.

The state-run hospitals in Estonia are hit-and-miss in terms of service, and most foreigners use them only if absolutely necessary. The standards at private clinics are much better, but these generally don't provide emergency services. If you have a medical problem, you can contact the **East Tallinn Central Hospital** (Ravi 18; www.itk.ee). If an ambulance is needed, call 112.

> Where's the nearest (all-night) pharmacy? **Kus on lähim (ööpäev lahti olev) apteek?**
> I need a doctor/dentist. **Ma vajan arsti/hambaarsti.**
> an ambulance **kiirabi**
> hospital **haigla**
> an upset stomach **kõht on korrast ära**
> I have a stomach ache/sunburn/a fever. **Minu kõht valutab/päikesepõletus/palavik.**

LANGUAGE

The national language is Estonian, a Finno-Ugric tongue related to Finnish and Hungarian but completely unrecognisable to Estonia's other neighbours. Its complicated grammatical structure and baffling vowels have given it the reputation of being one of the world's most difficult languages to learn. Fortunately, English is widely spoken in the capital, and you should have no trouble communicating.

> Do you speak English? **Kas te räägite inglise keelt?**
> Hello **Tere**
> Goodbye **Head aega/nägemist**
> Pardon me **Vabandust**
> Please **Palun**
> Thank you **Aitäh**

> Cheers! **Terviseks!**

LGBTQ+ TRAVELLERS

Attitudes towards homosexuality in Estonia are beginning to catch up with those in other European countries. Overt displays, such as holding hands, may attract attention but no more than in most of Western Europe, though many local people are less open about their sexuality. The website www.local-life.com/tallinn offers tips and advice to LGBTQ+ travellers and lists the city's handful of LGBTQ+ bars and clubs. X-Baar (Tatari 1) is the most established of these, but Club 69 (Sakala 24; www.club69.ee), a bar and sauna, is at least as popular.

MEDIA

Press. A handful of English-language city guides can be found in town, but the best of the bunch is the invaluable *Tallinn In Your Pocket* (www.inyourpocket.com/tallinn). The region's only English-language newspaper is the Riga-based weekly *The Baltic Times* (www.baltictimes.com). International newspapers can be found in major hotels and larger downtown kiosks.

Radio. Raadio Tallinn (103.5MHz FM; https://raadiotallinn.err.ee) re-broadcasts the BBC World Service daily. Pop music stations include Sky Plus (92.6MHz) and Power Hit Radio (102.1MHz).

Television. Estonia's three major broadcasters are the public Estonian National Broadcasting (ETV, ETV2, ETV+), the commercial Kanal2, which also runs channels 11 and 12, and TV3, which has a bevy of entertainment-style programmes on TV6. All have a number of imported shows in English.

MONEY

Estonia uses the euro (EUR). Banknotes come in denominations of 500, 200, 100, 50, 20, 10 and 5 euros, and coins in denominations of 2 and 1 euros, and 50, 20, 10, 5, 2 and 1 cents.

Currency exchange. A number of colourful, brightly lit currency exchanges dot Old Town but almost always offer fantastically bad rates. You will score a much better deal from any commercial bank such as Swedbank, SEB or Nordea. Otherwise, Tavid (Tartu mnt 87) operates a daily exchange window that will do in a necessity.

ATMs. These are never hard to come by in Tallinn, especially in the touristy Old Town.

Travellers' cheques. Travellers' cheques from major issuers such as Thomas Cook and American Express are exchangeable at most banks, but are not accepted as payment in shops, restaurants or hotels.

> Can I pay with this credit card? **Kas ma saan selle krediitkaardiga maksta?**
> I want to change some pounds/dollars. **Ma soovin vahetada naelasid/dollareid.**
> Can you cash a traveller's cheque? **Kas te saaksite reisitšekke rahaks vahetada?**
> Where's the nearest bank/currency exchange office? **Kus on lähim pank/valuutavahetus?**
> Is there a cash machine near here? **Kas lähedal on pangaautomaat?**
> How much is that? **Kui palju see maksab?**

OPENING TIMES

Opening hours vary from business to business, but most follow these general customs:

Banks are open 9am–5pm Monday to Friday, with some of the larger branches also open 10am–3pm on Saturday.

Museums are open 10am–6pm. Most are closed Monday or Tuesday.

Small shops open at 10am and close 5–7pm Monday to Friday. Some are closed Saturdays, but most open 10am–3 or 4pm. They are almost always closed Sundays. **Department stores** and **shopping centres**, on the other hand, stay open much later. These are open 9am–9pm daily, sometimes closing an hour or two earlier on Sundays.

Restaurants generally open at 11am or noon and close at 10–11pm. Some stay open one or two hours later on Friday and Saturday nights. Sundays are slow for restaurants, prompting a few to close their doors at 5–6pm. At weekends, the popular **bars** and **pubs** in the Old Town stay open until 2 or 3am.

POLICE

Estonia's national **Politsei**, seen roving the streets in dark-blue jumpsuits, are responsible for stopping crime and keeping order. Those assigned to the Old Town usually understand at least some English or will call a colleague who can. The green-clad **Munitsipaalpolitsei**, or municipal police, mainly issue fines for riding buses without tickets or violating city ordinances. If you find yourself in need of the police, call 112, or report crimes at the main police station at Kolde pst 65; tel: 6125 400.

> Where's the nearest police station? **Kus on lähim politseijaoskond?**
> I've lost my wallet/bag/passport. **Kaotasin oma rahakoti/koti/passi.**

POST OFFICE

Postal services are handled by Omniva (www.omniva.ee). To send home post or purchases, Tallinn's Kaubamaja Post Office, in the central shopping district, should be your first stop. It is open 10am–7pm Monday to Friday, 10am–3pm Saturday, and English-speakers are plentiful. Stamps are also sold in most kiosks and by many of the postcard vendors operating stands in Old Town. Drop your postcards and letters in any of the bright orange post boxes you see around town, or in the old-fashioned green boxes in Old Town. Both are decorated with Eesti Post's bugle symbol.

> Where's the nearest post office? **Kus on lähim postkontor?**
> express (special delivery) **kullerteenus registered**

PUBLIC HOLIDAYS

The following are public holidays in Estonia when banks, shops and offices are closed. Restaurants, cafés and bars usually close only on Christmas, New Year's Day and Midsummer.

New Year's Day 1 January
Independence Day (1918) 24 February
Good Friday and Easter March or April
Spring Day 1 May
Whitsunday 20 May
Victory Day 23 June
Midsummer Day (St John's Day) 24 June
Day of Restoration of Independence 20 August
Christmas 25 December
Boxing Day 26 December

TELEPHONES

To phone Estonia from abroad, dial your international access code (00 in the UK), Estonia's country code (372), and then the number as listed. There are no city codes to add or digits to drop.

When phoning abroad from Estonia, dial 00, then your country code. If you need information or assistance from an operator, or you want to connect to an operator in your own country, dial 1184. Direct access numbers to organisations like AT&T will allow you to make credit-card calls or, in some cases, to reverse the charges (call collect). AT&T: 80 012 001; MCI 80 012 122; Canadian Teleglobe 80 012 011; BT 80 010 442.

Roaming is possible with any mobile phone that uses the standard European band. To avoid roaming charges, you can invest in a local SIM card, available from most kiosks. The starter kits, sold under brand names such as Telia or Elisa, cost €5–8.

Public telephones have been phased out.

TIME ZONES

Estonia is in the Eastern European Time Zone. As in the UK, Daylight Saving Time is in effect from the last Sunday in March to the last Sunday in October. The following chart shows the time in various cities in summer.

San Francisco	New York	London	**Tallinn**	Sydney
2am	5am	10am	**noon**	7pm

TIPPING

Tipping in Estonia is somewhat haphazard. Some people tip, some do not. In restaurants you can reward good service with a ten percent tip, and it is best to do so in cash. Tips will not be expected for meals in simpler cafés, pubs, or anywhere you pay at the till. Taxi drivers do not get tips, but you can round up to the next euro. Hotel porters should get around €5, and tour guides for large groups are usually tipped around €5 by each person.

TOILETS

In Estonia the WC *(veetsee)* is sometimes marked using a baffling system of triangles. A triangle pointing downwards is the men's room, and one pointing up is the women's. Otherwise, men's and women's are marked *Meeste* (M) and *Naiste* (N), respectively. Public toilets, some of which used to appear in the form of coin-operated kiosks, are now free of charge. If out and about in Old Town, you can find them near the Viru Gates on Valli, in the underground walkway beneath Freedom Square and on Toompea next to the Alexander Nevsky Cathedral.

> Where are the toilets? **Kus on WC (veetsee)?**

TOURIST INFORMATION

The best place to find in-depth, authoritative information is the Tallinn Tourist Information Centre in the Old Town at Niguliste 2/Kullassepa 4 (9am–6pm; tel: 6457 777; www.visittallinn.ee). The Estonian Tourism Board provides general travel information on its website, www.visitestonia.com.

TRANSPORT

City transit. The united system of buses, trams and electric trolleybuses that makes up Tallinn's public transport system operates in general from 6am to 11pm. It is run by the TLT Company, whose website (www.tlt.ee) displays timetables, maps and a route planner in English. Maps posted on most bus stops will also show you how to make your journey, and you can call tel: 6434 142 during working hours for further info. Trams mainly service the centre of town, whereas the buses and trolleybuses will take you to outlying areas. Single-ride tickets can be bought from the driver for €2, but the most common way to pay is by contactless credit or debit card or by smartcard, an electronic card sold and reloaded in post offices and kiosks in varying denominations. There is a €1 fee for new cards. Board from any door and validate your ticket by touching one of the round validators with it. Each validation costs €2 and is good for one hour. In any given 24hr period you will never be charged more than the daily pass rate of €5.50. The system also works with contactless bank cards. Holders of the Tallinn Card, which is available from the Tourist Information Office (see page 138) and larger hotels, are entitled to unlimited free use of public transport (see page 126, and should validate their rides in the same manner.

Inter-city buses. Tallinn's bus station (Bussijaam; Lastekodu 46; www.tpilet.ee) is just outside the city centre and can be reached by trams No. 2 and 4. Its website lists all times and prices in English. Buses to St Petersburg, Riga and other international destinations are operated by Lux Express (www.luxexpress.eu), which has a separate office in the bus station.

Taxis. The biggest complaint among tourists is taxi drivers who overcharge. By law, all taxis are required to clearly state their rates, in English, on large yellow stickers on their right passenger windows. But there is no law saying that these rates cannot be exorbitant. Normal rates consist of a base fare of max €5.50 plus a per-kilometre charge of max €1.10. Be wary of anyone asking for more. You can order a taxi by phone for the same price as getting one on the street. A good, cheap company is Reval Takso (tel: 1207; www.reval-takso.ee). Otherwise, download a rideshare app like Uber or Bolt and pay by phone – both companies operate within the city.

Where can I get a taxi? **Kust ma saaksin takso?**
What's the fare to (the centre)? **Palju maksab (keslinna)?**
Take me to this address. **Viige mind sel aadressil.**
Where is the nearest bus stop? **Kus on lähim bussipeatus?**
When's the next bus to…? **Millal läheb järmine buss…?**
I want a ticket to… **Palun üks pilet…sse.**
single/return **üks suund/edasitagasi**
How much is a ticket to (Tartu)? **Palju maksab pilet (Tartusse)?**
Will you tell me when to get off? **Kas te ütlete millal, ma pean maha minema?**

VISA AND ENTRY REQUIREMENTS

Passports/visas. Estonia is a member of the Schengen common visa area, so travellers coming from other Schengen countries will almost never have to undergo immigration or customs checks when crossing the border. That said, the law still requires that everyone brings valid travel documents and is able to produce them if asked. For visiting EU and EEA citizens, the document can be just a national ID card, but for all others, a valid passport is needed. When entering from outside Schengen, the above documents will be checked.

UK passport-holders can enter Estonia freely, provided their passport has a 'date of issue' less than ten years before the date of arrival and an 'expiry date' at least three months from the departure date. Citizens of the US, Canada, Australia and New Zealand can enter the Schengen zone and stay for up to ninety days in a six-month period without a visa. South Africans require Schengen visas. Contact the nearest Schengen country consulate to enquire about application procedures.

Regulations can change, so always check before you travel.

Customs. When arriving from outside the EU, you can import the usual two hundred cigarettes, and one litre of hard alcohol or two litres of light alcohol (under 22 percent) without paying duties.

Exporting antiques. Antiques bought in Estonia cannot be exported without a permit. This applies to anything made in Estonia before 1945 and anything made elsewhere before 1850. Antique dealers should be able to assist you with the paperwork. Contact the National Heritage Board (tel: 6403 050; www.muinsuskaitseamet.ee) for information.

WEBSITES AND INTERNET

A few websites that will come in handy:

www.visittallinn.ee/eng The city's official tourism website, an excellent resource for travel planning.

www.visitestonia.com/en Estonia's official tourism website.

www.inyourpocket.com The extensive site of *Tallinn In Your Pocket*.

http://news.err.ee ERR News, by far the best source of daily local news in English.

www.vm.ee The Foreign Ministry's site, with interesting, general information on Estonia.

www.culture.ee A database of festivals and other events around the country.

www.ilm.ee Current weather conditions, as well as webcam views.

Free wi-fi is offered throughout the city. Nearly all cafés and restaurants have free wi-fi and there are also free public access points (you can see the map at: www.wifimap.io/en/65-estonia).

YOUTH HOSTELS

The **Estonian Youth Hostel Association** (www.hostels.ee) provides most of its booking services through its website. Not all of the prominent hostels are listed, however.

Old Town hostels cater mainly to backpackers looking for a party atmosphere. Chief among these is **The Monk's Bunk** (Lai 22; www.toth.ee). **Fat Margaret's** (Põhja pst 27; tel: 510 0916) is just outside Old Town. Not far away, **Euphoria Lounge and Rooms** (Roosikrantsi 4; tel: 5837 3602) is a good alternative.

Farther out, **Academic Hostel** (Akadeemia tee 11; tel: 6202 275; www.academichostel.com) is a large, modern hostel 5km (3 miles) from the city centre.

Index

A

Adamson-Eric Museum 36
Aegna 84
Alexander Nevsky Cathedral 36
Altja 81

B

Bastion Tunnels 40

C

Castle Square 35
Centre of Tallinn 50
children 103
Children's Museum Miiamilla 105
Church Square 42

D

Danish King's Garden 41
Dome Church (Cathedral of St Mary the Virgin) 42
Dominican Monastery (St Catherine's) 60
Draakon Gallery 55

E

Estonian Film Museum 76
Estonian History Museum 54, 76
Estonian Maritime Museum 59
Estonian Museum of Contemporary Art 70
Estonian Open Air Museum 79

F

Fat Margaret's Tower 59
festivals 105
Freedom Square 64

G

Governor's Garden 39
Great Coast Gate 59
Great Guild Hall 54

H

Haapsalu 90
Harju Hill 66
Hirve Park 66
Holy Spirit Church 51
House of the Brotherhood of Black Heads 56

J

Jägala Waterfall 83

K

Kadriorg 70
Kadriorg Art Museum 72
Kadriorg Palace 71
Kadriorg Park 73
Kalamaja 67
Kalev Marzipan Museum Room 53
Kanut Guild Hall 55
Käsmu 81
KGB Headquarters 57
Kiek in de Kök 39
Kohtu Street viewing platform 43

Kumu 72

L

Lahemaa National Park 80
Latin Quarter 60
Lembit submarine 69
Linda Hill 66
Linnahall 70
Long Leg Gate Tower 35
Lower Town 46
Lühike jalg 35

M

Maarjamäe 75
Maarjamäe War Memorial 75
Maiasmokk 53
Maiden's Tower 42
Männiku 83
Mikkel Museum 72
Museum of Estonian Architecture 71
Museum of Photography 49

N

Naissaar 83
nightlife 94
Niguliste Museum and Concert Hall 63

O

Old Thomas 48
Orthodox Cathedral 36

P

Palmse Manor 80

Parliament Building 38
Pärnu 84
Patarei Prison 68
Patkuli viewing platform 44
Pikk jalg 35
Pirita 76
Prangli 84
Prison Museum 68

R

Railway and Communications Museum 91
Rotermanni Salt Storage 71
Rotermann Quarter 71
Russalka Memorial 74

S

Sagadi Manor 81
Schnelli Pond 67
Seaplane Harbour 69
shopping 96
Short Leg Gate Tower 36
Song Festival Arena 75
Song Festival Grounds 75
sports 102
Square of Towers 67
Stable Tower 42
St Bridget's Convent 44, 76
St Catherine's (Dominican) Monastery 60
St Catherine's Guild 62
St Catherine's Passage 62
Stenbock House 45
St John's Church 65
St Nicholas Church 62
St Nicholas's Orthodox Church 60
St Olav's Church 57
Suur Tõll icebreaker 69
Swan Pond 73

T

Tall Hermann 39
Tallinn Botanical Gardens 76
Tallinn City Museum 60
Tallinn Song Festival Arena 44
Tallinn TV Tower 44, 77
Tallinn Zoo 79, 105
Tartu 87
Three Sisters 59
Toompark 67
Toompea 33
Toompea Castle 37
Town Hall 48
Town Hall Pharmacy 50
Town Hall Prison 49
Town Hall Square 47
Town Hall Tower 49
Town wall 44

V

Vabamu Museum of Occupations and Freedom 57
Viewing platforms 43
Viinistu 82
Viru Hotel and KGB Museum 57

W

War of Independence Victory Column 65

THE MINI ROUGH GUIDE TO
TALLINN

First edition 2025

Editor: Joanna Reeves
Author: Steve Roman
Updater: Ellen Himelfarb
Picture Editor: Piotr Kala
Picture Manager: Tom Smyth
Cartography Update: Katie Bennett
Layout: Grzegorz Madejak
Production Operations Manager: Katie Bennett
Publishing Technology Manager: Rebeka Davies
Head of Publishing: Sarah Clark
Photography Credits: All images **Shutterstock** except: Arno Mikkor 106; iStock 15C, 15T, 16TL, 16CL, 22, 38, 43, 46/47, 52, 66, 78, 81, 86, 90, 97, 100, 107; JoJan/Wikimedia Commons under CC BY-SA 4.0 license 24; Micah Sarut/Apa Publications 104, 108; Peeter Jahe 14CL; Public domain 23, 26, 28
Cover Credits: Toompea Hill **ESB Professional/Shutterstock**

About the author
Born in the United States, raised in Canada and now based in the UK, Ellen Himelfarb has led a life on the move. She's explored Western Africa, lived in China, island-hopped around the Norwegian Sea, and travelled the length and breadth of Estonia. Her writing appears regularly in British broadsheet newspapers and magazines, including National Geographic Traveller (UK) – as well as the Canadian press. In addition to updating the Rough Guide Mini Tallinn, Ellen contributed to the brand-new Rough Guide to Slow Travel in Europe. Find Ellen online @ellenhimelfarb.

Distribution
UK, Ireland and Europe: Apa Publications (UK) Ltd; mail@roughguides.com
United States and Canada: Two Rivers; ips@ingramcontent.com
Australia and New Zealand: Woodslane; info@woodslane.com.au
Worldwide: Apa Publications (UK) Ltd; mail@roughguides.com

Special Sales, Content Licensing and CoPublishing
Rough Guides can be purchased in bulk quantities at discounted prices. We can create special editions, personalized jackets and corporate imprints tailored to your needs.
mail@roughguides.com
roughguides.com

EU Representative
LOGOS EUROPE, 9 rue Nicolas Poussin, 17000, LA ROCHELLE, France; Contact@logoseurope.eu; +33 (0) 667937378

Printed by Finidr in Czech Republic

ISBN: 9781835291849

This book was produced using **Typefi** automated publishing software.

A catalogue record for this book is available from the British Library

All Rights Reserved
© 2025 Apa Digital AG
License edition © Apa Publications Ltd UK

No part of this book may be reproduced, stored in a retrieval system, or transmitted in any form or by any means – electronic, mechanical, photocopying, recording, or otherwise – without prior written permission from Apa Publications.

No part of this book may be used or reproduced in any manner for the purpose of training artificial intelligence technologies or systems.

Contact us
Every effort has been made to ensure that this publication is accurate, free from safety risks, and provides accurate information. However, changes and errors are inevitable. The publisher is not responsible for any resulting loss, inconvenience, injury or safety concerns arising from the use of this book. If you notice any errors, outdated information, or potential safety risks, please send your comments with the subject line "Rough Guide Mini Tallinn Update" to mail@roughguides.com.

Things to Spot in Winter

Illustrated by
Di Brookes

Designed by Jenny Addison
Words by Simon Tudhope and Sarah Russell

There's a chart with stickers at the back of the book
to help you keep track of the things you have seen.

Gardens

Winter honeysuckle
Bursts into bloom late in the year. You might catch the sweet scent of its flowers as you walk past.

Common beech
This thick hedge has a warm, coppery glow in the winter sun. Its dry leaves rustle as little birds dart about inside.

Eats fruit, seeds, insects and worms

Robin
A bold little bird with a rusty red breast. Listen out for its sweet, high song.